ANXIETY
ELEPHANTS
FOR TWEEN GIRLS

A 90 DAY DEVOTIONAL

CARIS SNIDER

Anxiety Elephants for Tween Girls

End Game Press books may be purchased in bulk at special discounts for sales promotion, corporate gifts, ministry, fund-raising, or educational purposes. Special editions can also be created to specifications. For details, contact Special Sales Dept., End Game Press, P.O. Box 206, Nesbit, MS 38651 or info@endgamepress.com.

Visit our website at www.endgamepress.com

Library of Congress Control Number: 2021948263
ISBN: 978-1-63797-015-7
eBook ISBN: 978-1-63797-016-4

Cover Design by Christopher Gilbert, Gilbert & Carlson Design, LLC
Interior design by Typewriter Creative Co.

Printed in India
TPL
10 9 8 7 6 5 4 3 2 1

Dedicated to: Zoe and Allye

Thank you for giving mom the encouragement to write a book for your generation.

Love you!

CONTENTS

ANXIETY SYMPTOMS

In preparing for this book, I did a survey asking tweens to share symptoms they feel when the Anxiety Elephants come. I am sharing below to bring awareness for parents and to help other tweens, like you, know you are not alone in your experience. You may discover you have felt all these symptoms or only a couple. It could be very possible what you experience is not listed here. Go through the list and select which ones stand out. Write in other symptoms you have experienced not already listed.

- Headache
- Stomachache
- Dizziness
- Rapid Heart Rate
- Feeling Breathless
- Insomnia
- Sweaty Palms
- Uncontrollable outbursts of anger or sadness
- Fear
- Constant Worry
- Fidgeting
- Not able to get words out
- Difficulty concentrating at school, sports activities, etc.

For a list of more symptoms of anxiety for tweens, go to: https://kidshealth.org

INTRODUCTION

The rumbling...do you hear it? Can you feel it? You are walking into school, getting ready to shoot the ball, or picking up your pencil for a test, and here they come—Anxiety Elephants.

You know the feeling, right? They sneak around in the bushes waiting for the right moment to strike. At this point, it's too late. There is nothing you can do to stop them. Suddenly, they pounce. A herd of elephants jump up and down on your chest.

If you struggle with what I've described, know you are not alone. I hid my struggle against anxiety for a long time. I thought Anxiety Elephants, as I like to call them, only attacked me. I didn't know there were others who struggled with the same thing.

Growing up, I dealt with a lot of anxiety, but I didn't know what it was. When I would get bullied or be afraid of something, my heart would race, or I couldn't sleep at night. Sometimes trying to get one breath out was exhausting. I will never forget in fifth grade waking up with blurry vision and extreme headaches. I told my parents my symptoms, and they took me to the doctor. He asked if I was being bullied. He mentioned anxiety, and I was relieved to know what was happening inside my body. However, he didn't give me any solutions I could use to cope with and overcome my problems.

Over the next ninety days, I want to give you what I wish someone would have given me to help stomp out those Anxiety Elephants. You will find scripture, tools, journaling pages to write your thoughts, and stomp steps.

Anxiety uses repetition to attack. It doesn't use a million different messages to invade your life—the lies are always the same. In the following pages, you will find truth repeated to break the hold of untruths looping in your mind.

Anxiety will not be allowed to overcome you. As you open each day, you will be equipped to do the overcoming. There will be some simple skills and some others a little more difficult. You may find certain days of stomping out Anxiety Elephants will feel a little silly. I hope laughter comes through those pages.

Now, are you ready to stomp? Let's go!

ONE

The light shines in the darkness, and the
darkness has not overcome it.

John 1:5, ESV

Light is a powerful source of energy. You can walk into a pitch-dark room, unable to see two steps in front of you. When the door opens, the smallest sliver of light changes everything. All the furniture surrounding you is no longer hidden. Or, you could be outside camping with your buddies. All of a sudden, you hear the howl of an animal close to your tents. Shaky hands grab the flashlight to see what is lurking in the dark. A baby raccoon is revealed in the shining beam. The darkness played tricks on your eyes until the light showed the truth.

Light always overcomes darkness. You are now learning how to turn it on.

Think of this devotional like a flashlight in your toolkit. Just as you use a flashlight to push back the darkness, this book can be used in the same way. The more you learn, the brighter the light gets. As God's Word takes root in your heart and practical skills are put into place, the shadows of Anxiety Elephants will begin to fade away.

Some days will be easier than others. That is normal. This will be a daily process of small steps. Each one will be huge no matter how it appears. Spend extra time in God's Word today and allow His light to drown out the darkness of anxiety.

STOMP STEPS

Grab some flashlights, family, and friends and go play flashlight tag! Think on how big the light of God is in your life.

PRAYER

Thank you, God, for being stronger than the darkness of anxiety!

JOURNAL

....

....

....

....

....

....

....

....

....

....

....

TWO

Come to me, all who are weary and
burdened, and I will give you rest.

Matthew 11:28, NASB

Anxiety Elephants—where in the world do they come from?

At your age, anxiety made it very hard for me to enjoy life. My heart would beat at a scary speed. For what felt like hours, the heaviest feeling I had ever experienced weighed me down leaving me breathless.

Close your eyes and imagine a herd of elephants running towards you as fast as they can. Picture them jumping on top of your chest like a trampoline, and they just—won't—stop. This is what an anxiety attack feels like!

From the start, I hid my anxiety behind a smile. Finding relief was a huge desire of my heart, but admitting I needed it was the biggest barrier to overcome. I didn't know there were others struggling with Anxiety Elephants.

Knowing that I could come to Jesus with all my burdens changed things.

No matter what you do, you may still have moments where the breath is knocked out of you as Anxiety Elephants kick you into a cloud of dust and make you feel like you're landing on the hard, cold ground—I do. Our scripture gives us a powerful reminder. When you experience these kinds of attacks, Jesus invites you to come and find rest in His supernatural peace.

STOMP STEP

The very first thing I had to do when facing my
anxiety was confess and pray. What do you want
God to know you have been hiding from Him?

PRAYER

Dear God, I have decided to no longer hide from you. Please
forgive me for trying to do this on my own. I need You. I
need the tools You have available for me to overcome.

JOURNAL

....

....

....

....

....

....

....

....

....

....

THREE

That is why, for Christ's sake, I delight in weaknesses,
in insults, in hardships, in persecutions, in difficulties.
For when I am weak, then I am strong.

2 Corinthians 12:10, NIV

When really hard things happen to you, it sticks in your heart forever. In first grade, a boy in my classroom gathered everyone around to make fun of me. I was born with a mild form of cerebral palsy causing the muscles in my left arm to be really tight and my foot was turned inward. He held his arms up like a bunny rabbit and began to hop around me saying that is what I looked like.

Pretty harsh, right?

I went home and cried but told no one. It looked like this 'friend' used my weakness against me. I thought to not be made fun of again, I had to be perfect and never show my weaknesses.

I was mistaken. We do not have to hide struggles like anxiety and pretend to have it all together. We can be open and honest about our imperfections with God.

He can handle any difficult situation. Nothing is too hard for Him. The Lord's strength comes shining out in our weaknesses. As we allow Him into those places, they no longer have power over us; we have power over them.

STOMP STEP

Share a moment someone made fun of you. Talk to your
parents or an adult you trust about this experience and ask
for their help in finding God's strength to move forward.

PRAYER

Dear Lord, help me to remember Your strength
will shine through my weakness.

JOURNAL

....

....

....

....

....

....

....

....

....

....

....

FOUR

Go now, write it on a tablet for them, inscribe it on a scroll,
that for the days to come it may be an everlasting witness.

Isaiah 30:8, NIV

Writing things down, journaling, never really sounded like fun to me. I couldn't understand how putting things down on paper could be helpful. Surely there were other things to do with a little more fun attached. Then, I tried it one day.

I had an old notebook with some blank pages left. I opened it and started moving my pen. At first, words came out in a line, single file. Eventually, sentences began to flow. Just letting the ink move without worry of punctuation and correct spelling felt freeing. The focus was to get out everything coming to my mind at the moment.

Something was different. Journaling allowed me to feel lighter. It opened my eyes to how much pain I had been carrying around every day. Looking back on those pages now, I realize all the work God has done and the victories that have taken place.

By using the Journal section, you will have an opportunity to look back and see the change God is doing in your life. Writing it all out erases the path Anxiety Elephants are using against you. You can freely let go of every burden. Putting the hidden words on paper will put change in your heart.

STOMP STEP

Practice letting the words out. Start with doodling until the sentences come. Don't hold back anything wanting to come out.

PRAYER

Help me to try this new thing, God. Give me
the freedom to let the words flow.

JOURNAL

....

....

....

....

....

....

....

....

....

....

....

FIVE

But it is the spirit in a person, the breath of the
Almighty, that gives them understanding.

Job 32:8, NIV

Breathing is a powerful thing. Not in the sense your sister's breath is so strong it knocks you backwards every morning. I mean it is important to every part of you. In fact, it was one thing God used to put creation into existence.

God spoke most of the world and universe into being. We read in the very first chapter of Genesis, "Let there be light," and there was light. God did this for the trees, animals, water, and sky. For man, He did something different. He breathed His breath of life into Adam, and he became a living creature.

WHOA. . .the breath of God is in us!

Even my smart watch knows how valuable breathing is. It goes off at least once a day to remind me to breathe so I can focus.

By taking deep breaths in through your nose and exhaling out through your mouth, it works like the light switches in your house. The movement of air through your lungs causes the thinking part of your brain to turn on and take control. This is where clear thoughts happen. By being in the thinking part of your brain, you turn the emotional part off when anxiety wants to take charge.

You don't have to hold your breath anymore waiting for the next attack. Take control of your breathing and let the Almighty's breath fill your life.

STOMP STEP

Practice deep breathing. A few times throughout the day, take a deep breath in your nose and slowly breathe out of your mouth. Hold the breath in for several seconds. The more you practice, the more calm you will experience.

PRAYER

Thank you, God, for breathing your breath in my lungs.

JOURNAL

....

....

....

....

....

....

....

....

....

....

....

SIX

"My soul is overwhelmed with sorrow to the
point of death," he said to them.

Mark 14:34a, NIV

How did Jesus deal with the overwhelm?

My mouth hit the floor the first time I read this passage seeing the words Jesus spoke. Knowing our Savior has experienced what being overwhelmed feels like brought a sigh of relief.

He didn't hide. Jesus made it very clear how He was feeling. He didn't push it down and hide behind "I'm good," "I'm fine," or "#blessed"!

Jesus told His friends, James, Peter, and John, to go a little further with Him in the garden. He wanted His friends close in His time of need. Your friends can't prevent you from feeling overwhelmed, but they can help you walk through it.

Jesus prayed. He went to His Father and laid it all out. He called God, *ABBA*. This word is an Aramaic word meaning "Daddy." Jesus was close to God and knew He could go to Him with what was going on. By doing this, He shows us we can do the same. If you continue reading this passage of scripture, Jesus prayed two more times leaning closer into His Father's love. It was not a one and done prayer.

We see God didn't tell Jesus to suck it up or get back to work. He met Jesus there in that moment. He will do the same for you in the middle of your distress. He got Jesus to the other side, and His strength will do the same for you.

STOMP STEP

Follow the example of Jesus. Spend time on your
knees and have a heart-to-heart talk with God.

PRAYER

If Jesus can be honest with you, God, so will
I. Here is how I am feeling today.

JOURNAL

....

....

....

....

....

....

....

....

....

....

....

SEVEN

If any of you lacks wisdom, let him ask God, who gives generously to all without reproach, and it will be given him.

James 1:5, ESV

All in favor of getting rid of tests, raise your hand! My sixteen-year-old self felt this the day I failed my driver's license test. Heart racing, palms sweating, and breath, well I couldn't breathe. The instructor said turn left. I heard her, but my mind told me to turn right. She yelled. I cried. It was horrible. Mercy was given, and I was allowed to take the test over. I passed, but no one knew I failed the first time. Actually, you guys are now in on my secret.

I thought I was the only one who struggled with any type of test.

Are tests hard for you? Do you study and prepare, only to find yourself going blank at the sight of the first question? Test anxiety is a real thing, not made up in your head. It can block your brain from thinking clearly and emotions take over, keeping you from answering.

How can you deal with test anxiety? Our scripture tells us to ask God for wisdom. Talking to God about a test is not too small for Him. If the test is important to you, it is important to Him.

Instead of waiting until the night before the test, change your habit and study in small pieces leading up to it. When test day arrives, take a deep breath. Exhale the worry and ask God to give you wisdom. All you can do is your best and trust Him with the rest.

STOMP STEP

Tell your parents or your teachers about how tests make you feel.

PRAYER

Thank you, God, for caring about everything, including my tests.

JOURNAL

....

....

....

....

....

....

....

....

....

....

....

EIGHT

I waited patiently for the Lord; he turned to me and heard my cry. He lifted me out of the slimy pit, out of the mud and mire; he set my feet on a rock and gave me a firm place to stand.

Psalms 40:1-2, NIV

Do you remember a time in your life where you got stuck? I never got my head stuck anywhere, but my pinky was another story. There was this tiny, blue vase with pink flowers I found for my Mom during the school book fair. What, you never bought something other than books?

I thought the opening looked big enough to fit my pinky. Wrong! Panic set in, and I started swinging this colorful piece of clay as fast as I could. The next thing I heard was pieces shattering.

Anxiety makes us feel the same way. When that elephant comes and plops down on your chest, a crushing feeling takes over and pushes you down. The harder you try to get out from under it, the more confused you become. You feel weighed down almost like you are in a pit of quicksand.

How do you get out?

Treat it like real quicksand. Quicksand is a dense mixture of water and sand that forms into a solid appearing, sinking substance. When you step into it, your feet slowly sink down. If you panic, it can cause you to go down faster. Researchers suggest the best way to get out of quicksand is to do the following: relax, take deep breaths, retreat slowly, rest, and repeat.

Try these steps the next time anxious feelings ambush you. By following this process, you will begin to feel God lifting you up and putting your feet on firm ground.

STOMP STEP

Make your own quicksand. As you stick your
fingers in, practice using the steps above: relax,
take deep breaths, move slowly, and repeat.

1 cup of water
1.5 to 2 cups cornstarch

PRAYER

Thank you, God, for listening to me. It is good to know how
much you love and care about everything in my life.

JOURNAL

....

....

....

....

....

....

....

....

....

....

NINE

Be strong and courageous. Do not fear or be in
dread of them, for it is the Lord your God who goes
with you. He will not leave you or forsake you.

Deuteronomy 31:6, ESV

The heavy feeling on your chest is back. You were trying to finish the math assignment, and pressure is building up on you. Breathing is hard. Air going in and out has moved from a steady flow to a rapid rhythm. Your heart beats as if it might jump out of your chest at any moment. Butterflies are swarming in your stomach. Palms are dripping in sweat.

"What is happening to me? Am I sick? Am I dying? Do I tell my parents? Are my friends going to make fun of me? Will this be something the bully uses to pick on me? Will the teachers listen? Does God care?"

Can you relate to these symptoms and questions? How can you be strong and courageous in the midst of feeling frozen during the real battle going on in your heart and mind?

Embrace God's presence by sitting and talking to Him through prayer. It is more powerful than the heavy feeling anxiety brings. When Moses spoke these words from our scripture to the Israelites, he is reminding them God would go before them and fight their battles not leaving them for a second. God is doing the same for you.

Keep moving. Put your pencil on the paper and work on one math problem at a time. Take a deep breath to put your heart back in a slower rhythm. Wash your hands and shake off the sweat. Drink some water to settle your stomach. Remind yourself God is near when Anxiety Elephants want to paralyze you in fear.

STOMP STEP

Write how anxiety makes you feel. In bold letters over
your list, write the words STRONG and COURAGEOUS as
a reminder of who you are through God's presence.

PRAYER

Dear God, anxiety makes me feel scared and I don't like it. Help
me have courage and remember You are always with me.

JOURNAL

....

....

....

....

....

....

....

....

....

....

....

TEN

I praise you because I am fearfully and wonderfully
made; your works are wonderful, I know that full well.

Psalms 139:14, NIV

You are *AWESOME!*

God made every part of you amazing which includes your brain.
It performs different connections making you move, breathe,
and think. In your brain, there are two important almond-shaped
amygdala which sounds like this: (A-mig-da-la). The two amygdala
are responsible for processing responses and memories associated
with fear and emotion. Here's an example of how this could be used:

Pretend there is a car speeding towards you. While this is happening,
you are in the middle of building the greatest Minecraft house ever
and suddenly, look up! What do you do? Run? "Fight" the car? Freeze?
This is when the amygdala come in handy. It is where your Fight or
Flight response lives. You will feel the adrenaline rushing through
your body to make your legs run as fast as possible.

Sometimes, the amygdala acts more like an overprotective parent.
Do any of you have one of those? They know how important you are
so even the thought of something being dangerous is treated like a
real-life scary situation. Anxiety comes into play causing panic in
your body over a thought, even if it's not a real thing.

Even when your brain goes into overdrive, God is not upset with you.
When the Fight, Flight, or Freeze response turns on when it isn't
needed, stop in your tracks and remember how AWESOME you are.

STOMP STEP

Draw these three words in a creative way: I AM AWESOME.
Here comes the hard part; choose to believe them.

PRAYER

Thank you, God, for helping me see how awesome you think I am!

JOURNAL

....

....

....

....

....

....

....

....

....

....

....

ELEVEN

Cast all your anxiety on him because he cares for you.

1 Peter 5:7, NIV

When I was your age, we went to my grandparents' house to fish. My Grandfather made sure the hooks were baited with wiggly worms and the catfish were ready to snag. We would cast our line over and over until the big one was caught!

Fishermen during biblical times cast their nets like this. Imagine them in their rowboat leaving the shore. Their job was to catch as many fish as possible. All day they would throw out the net, pull it in, empty it, and hurl it out again.

When anxious thoughts enter in causing you to feel overwhelmed, worried, or afraid, take on the mindset of a fisherman.

First, you need a net or fishing rod. This can be pen and paper or the note section on your phone. When a thought enters your mind making you feel uneasy, write it down as fast as you can. Next, rip the paper into pieces. Find the garbage and cast it; throw it away. If you use your phone, once you have completed the note, delete it.

Getting rid of these beginning seeds of anxiety keeps them from taking over your mind and holding you hostage in fear. God cares about what is going on in your mind. What do you need to tell Him today?

STOMP STEP

Write or draw one conversation you have over and over in your mind you want God to remove.

PRAYER

Thank you, God, for helping me get rid of thoughts
making me feel a little down and scared.

JOURNAL

....

....

....

....

....

....

....

....

....

....

....

TWELVE

Jesus wept.

John 11:35, NIV

I used to think crying was a bad thing. To keep the tears at bay, I would bite my lip as hard as I could so no one would see. If there was a bathroom close by, I would run and hide in a stall. When the tears did creep through, the embarrassment felt painful. For some reason, I thought being sad or upset was wrong.

Jesus shows us it is ok to cry.

Crying is not a sign of weakness. Being sad is not a sin. Feeling upset or having a bad day happens. You don't have to put pressure on yourself to appear to be happy and to have it together all the time.

If you read all of the story in John 11, Jesus had lost his friend, Lazarus, and He was grieving. He was also weeping because of the great disbelief in the hearts of those around Mary and Martha, the sisters of Lazarus. They didn't believe Jesus could raise him from the dead. He proved them all wrong.

If Jesus can cry, you can too. Do you have something in your life you need to grieve? Have you lost a friend? Are you moving? Have the homework assignments piled up and you feel like you are drowning under math facts? Is there a difficult situation going on at school? Are you getting ready to play a big rival and the pressure to perform well is coming from all directions? Is your family going through a challenging time?

Let the tears flow and release the anxiety of keeping it all together.

STOMP STEP

Time for a good cry.

PRAYER

Thank you, Jesus, for showing me it is ok to cry.

JOURNAL

....

....

....

....

....

....

....

....

....

....

....

THIRTEEN

Do not be anxious about anything, but in
every situation, by prayer and petition, with
thanksgiving, present your requests to God.

Philippians 4:6, NIV

Did you know our brains cannot be anxious and thankful at the same time? This attitude of gratitude will trigger feel-good hormones in your body called serotonin and dopamine which block negative thoughts from being in charge.

By concentrating on positive things, you are rewiring your brain and teaching it what to focus on. The Lord knows the power of gratitude. He tells us to bring *every* situation to Him by prayer and thanksgiving. So, how does this work?

You are already good at doing this. Adults can learn something from you about being thankful. When an anxious thought sneaks in, do a mental thankful checklist. Get as specific as possible. Tell God how thankful you are for your parents, friends who share their snack with you, or your scooter shooting sparks when you put on the breaks. As you enter into prayer with thanksgiving, ask God to help you with whatever stressful situation you are facing. His peace will come and quiet your mind bringing your heart back to a calm beat.

STOMP STEP

How many things can you think of today you are grateful
for? See if you can name more than your parents.

PRAYER

Thank you, God, for showing me how to pray if I feel anxious.
I want to tell you I am thankful for (fill in the blank).

JOURNAL

....

....

....

....

....

....

....

....

....

....

....

FOURTEEN

Finally, brothers and sisters, whatever is true, whatever
is noble, whatever is right, whatever is pure, whatever
is lovely, whatever is admirable—if anything is excellent
or praiseworthy—think about such things.

Philippians 4:8, NIV

Not too long ago, I would watch a crime show on TV before going to bed. It was a fiction story based on real situations. This was not the smartest move on my part. Something changed in my brain causing me to enter the *What If Zone.*

Maybe you have found yourself in the *What If Zone:* What if I get made fun of today? What if my friends don't want to be friends anymore? What if I stand up in front of the class and my zipper is unzipped? What if I fail this test? What if I don't get likes on my social media post? What if...fill in the blank.

This is not a fun place mentally. It is scary to constantly think about bad things happening.

What is causing you to think in an anxious place and how do you turn it off?

By switching off the *What If Zone,* you can now enter the *What IS Zone.* This place is filled with our verse today. Here, you discover things to focus on that are good, pure, and true. Staying in this region will keep your brain calm, and it will thank you for doing your part in exiting unhealthy territory.

STOMP STEP

What is one thing you need to no longer watch on TV, play in a video game, or interact with on social media? It will be a process to remove this from your life, but you can do it.

PRAYER

God, I don't want to put these things in my mind anymore. They make me feel yucky. Help me to focus on What IS and not What IF.

JOURNAL

....

....

....

....

....

....

....

....

....

....

....

FIFTEEN

The Lord is near to the brokenhearted
and saves the crushed in spirit.

Psalms 34:18, ESV

The constant pounding.

The constant berating.

The constant attacks.

The constant stomping.

It is a crushing feeling. The Anxiety Elephants come in undetected by anyone else around you. Punching you, pounding you, verbally attacking you. You might look like you are standing tall on the outside, but you are crushed into a million different pieces inside.

While all of this is happening, no one knows. No one hears the cries you barely let out. No one feels what you feel. Loneliness is the message Anxiety Elephants spew out convincing you no one cares. Is there anyone out there who really understands what you are going through?

At my lowest point, this verse cracked the window open to my soul. I cried because it was as if God was reaching down and holding my face between His two gentle hands saying, "I'm here and I love you." Close your eyes and imagine God is sitting in the room right now beside you doing the same for you.

God has more for you. He doesn't want you to be in that place any longer experiencing pain alone. Jesus came for the sick and hurting which means you and me. He is near. Open up to Him today.

STOMP STEP

Close your eyes, sit, or kneel. Your Good Father wants
to be the lifter of your head. He is cupping your face
in His hands right now and saying, "I love you."

PRAYER

Father, I need your love today. I am asking you to pull me
close to you. Lift my head and wipe away my tears.

JOURNAL

....

....

....

....

....

....

....

....

....

....

SIXTEEN

Say to those with fearful hearts, "Be strong, do not
fear; your God will come, he will come with vengeance;
with divine retribution he will come to save you."

Isaiah 35:4, NIV

When I was in the third grade, I cried so bad on a kiddie roller coaster they stopped it so I could get off and stop ruining the experience for the other children. As a teenager, I fake-fainted because I didn't want to go through the haunted house with my friends. I was too scared to tell them I was afraid. The memory of the emergency worker carrying me out still plays through my mind. My dad worked for the railroad, so when he was gone at night, I would be fearful without having him there. Even going to the dentist still causes me to get anxious.

Fear filled my heart all the time and I didn't know what to do with it. I never told anyone it was there. It is a lonely place being by yourself in fear.

Have you experienced fear like this? You might relate to some of the examples given, or maybe fear comes to you in different situations. Either way, it can still lead to a sad place.

Our verse reminds us to call on God and He will save in those fearful moments. Prayer is our way of calling out to God. It is our lifeline we can use day or night. Talking to Jesus about fear is the right thing to do. It opens the door to let Him come in and help you.

STOMP STEP

What are your fears? Write them below. Read Isaiah 35:4 and remind yourself these fears are powerless when God is your help.

PRAYER

Please help me with my fears, Jesus.

JOURNAL

....

....

....

....

....

....

....

....

....

....

....

SEVENTEEN

I can do all things through him who strengthens me.

Philippians 4:13, ESV

There is one sport I really loved growing up. . .basketball.

My brother and his friends would always include me in the game because I never really liked walking around the track talking. The ball would come my way quite a bit to shoot. Defense was never my favorite, but I would go hard when needed.

The time came to try out for the middle school team and eventually high school. I would love to tell you I tried out, broke records, and was the MVP, but my story ends here.

The anxiety I felt about playing in front of people and the pressure of winning and losing caused my heart to race out of my chest. I was afraid people would make fun of me because of my cerebral palsy. Knowing what rejection and embarrassment felt like, I never tried out. Would I have been good? Well, we will never know.

Anxiety stole from me and is trying to steal from you. God has strengthened you to do all things. This includes the very thing you are scared to do. What do you love to do, but anxiety has paralyzed you with fear? The only way to make fear disappear is to face it. Jesus is ready to give you the bravery to go forward. As you move ahead, your fear begins to shrink—and Jesus' power within you becomes greater.

STOMP STEP

What is one thing you love to do, but anxiety has tried to steal it from you? Ask a friend to help you face your fear and give it a try.

PRAYER

Thank you, Jesus, for giving me strength.
Help me to live with no regrets.

JOURNAL

....

....

....

....

....

....

....

....

....

....

....

....

EIGHTEEN

For he will command his angels concerning
you to guard you in all your ways.

Psalms 91:11, ESV

I was scared of the dark when I was your age. . .who am I kidding, I am still scared of the dark as an adult! Dogs barking late at night, trains blaring, and the house creaking. Up until college, I slept with a clown night light holding balloons. He was a friendly face to see as I got under the covers.

Bedtime anxiety happens for many your age. You go from being active and around people all day to dark silence. Your parents close the door and say, "sweet dreams", and your thoughts are far from sweet. You hear the stomping feet in your ears and see Anxiety Elephants pounding on your heart. You pull the blanket up tight until you can't take it anymore.

Some yell out in fear. Others wet the bed to have a reason to call a parent into the room. Many children hide under the covers until exhaustion sets in and their eyes finally close.

There is no judgement or shaming here for how Anxiety Elephants attack you and cause you to react at night. I remember.

Changing your nightly room environment is a solution to put into motion. Try sleeping with a light on. There are several LED options safe to leave on while you sleep. Find glow-in-the-dark stars to stick on your ceiling. Read a great book. Play worship music to keep your mind on the Lord. Use a notebook to draw and allow creativity to flow until your mind falls asleep.

Hold onto this verse when night comes and remember God's angels are surrounding you.

STOMP STEP

Write or draw one thing you would like to change during bed time tonight. Tell your parents and begin making these impactful changes for your night time routine.

PRAYER

Thank you, God, for your angels protecting me.

JOURNAL

....

....

....

....

....

....

....

....

....

....

....

NINETEEN

Bear one another's burdens, and so fulfill the law of Christ.

Galatians 6:2, ESV

There is one word we all find difficulty using. One word plagues adults and kids. It is a life-changing word when we put it into action. Our enemy knows it will shift the very direction life is going. What is this powerful word?

HELP

We convince ourselves we are supposed to figure it all out on our own. If we have problems or things are messing up, no one can know. People have enough to deal with in their own lives so we shouldn't burden them with our troubling situations.

Lies. . .it's all lies, friends!

God wants other people walking beside us; walking beside you. Helpers come in all forms. Counselors, doctors, teachers, parents, friends, pastors, and coaches are all people God has gently placed in your life to give you guidance and support. I know it's hard, but today is the day. . .it's time to put those four letters into action.

STOMP STEP

If you and your parents are walking through this devotional together, tell them how they can help you. If you are reading through these words alone, find an adult God has placed in your life to talk about hard things.

PRAYER

Lord, today I choose to reach out for help.

JOURNAL

....

....

....

....

....

....

....

....

....

....

....

TWENTY

When you lie down, you will not be afraid; when
you lie down, your sleep will be sweet.

Proverbs 3:24, NIV

Sleep! Where are you?!? I look for you night after night and you are nowhere to be found. Why have you left me?

Raise your hand if you struggle with going to sleep. It is frustrating, especially when you have a big test or project you need to be prepared for, but your mind is exhausted. You want to close your eyes and drift off to Sleepy Town, but the harder you try, the farther away it retreats. You find yourself avoiding bedtime because your mind races with thoughts of tasks you didn't complete. Then, your heart beats to the pounding of a herd of elephants moving through the African savanna.

Sweet sleep sounds nice, but how do you get there?

Instead of watching scary things on TV, find shows filled with joy and light-hearted fun. Laughter really is medicine for your soul. Spend time in worship and prayer, allowing God's powerful love to melt the anxieties in your heart. Write down your anxious thoughts so that they will stop bombarding your mind. Release them to God in prayer. Drinking sleepy-time tea and taking an Epsom salt bath will help close your tired eyes.

Rest in the truth that God handles all of your cares and concerns, and nothing you face will happen out of His sight. Write down this scripture and others to focus your mind and heart on God and not on all the events of the day. God's Word is a very powerful source for every area of your life, including sleep.

It's time for sleep to come back home to you.

STOMP STEP

Do a quick internet search for scriptures on sleep.
Write them down and pick one to focus on and
memorize before you drift off in sweet sleep.

PRAYER

God, I am really tired. I need help getting rest.
I am asking you for sweet sleep.

JOURNAL

....

....

....

....

....

....

....

....

....

....

TWENTY-ONE

We demolish arguments and every pretension that sets
itself up against the knowledge of God, and we take
captive every thought to make it obedient to Christ.

2 Corinthians 10:5, NIV

Anxiety Elephants can take your thoughts to some frightening places. Once they get planted in your head, they take over and trigger an entire sequence of unfortunate events. Before you know it, you are in complete panic mode, unable to breath, unable to move, unable to speak. All this stems from one single thought.

Our minds are powerful. What we think about affects every part of our lives. This is how anxiety can have such a strong hold. The more we cover up anxious thoughts, the bigger they become.

How can you change your daily thoughts?

STOP. Stop by taking action or say *stop* in your head. You get to be in charge of your brain.

After you **STOP** anxious thoughts from taking root, take them **CAPTIVE.** One way to capture anxious thoughts is to write all of your feelings down. Write until you can no longer hear your fears.

Finally, **REPLACE** old thoughts with new ones. If we don't put something else in our minds, we are left with empty space. Say life-giving thoughts out loud so your mind hears the shift you have made in your heart.

Overcoming anxiety is not an overnight fix. Once you get the hang of taking thoughts captive, it will happen so quickly the Anxiety Elephants won't know what hit them.

STOMP STEP

Write a new, positive thought and read it
out loud. Read it and believe it!

PRAYER

Lord, help me to take bad thoughts captive and
replace them with life-giving truth!

JOURNAL

....

....

....

....

....

....

....

....

....

....

....

TWENTY-TWO

But the Lord God called to the man, "Where are
you?" He answered, "I heard you in the garden, and
I was afraid because I was naked; so I hid."

Genesis 3:9-10, NIV

Did you know we have been hiding since the beginning of time?
Early on, Adam and Eve hid in the Garden of Eden. When the serpent,
the devil, convinced them to eat fruit God told them not to eat, they
realized they were naked! (Did anyone giggle reading the word
naked? It is ok, I did too.)

They didn't realize this until they sinned, and their eyes were opened.
God was in the garden looking for them and Adam said, "I was afraid,
so I hid." Fear caused them to hide.

Even though they were hiding, God was searching for them. He called
out to Adam and Eve. He is calling out to you.

Facing the fear you have of Anxiety Elephants attacking you could be
one of the hardest things you have ever done. I remember the first
time I told people I was dealing with anxiety. My biggest fear was
that they would reject me and turn their backs on me.

The opposite happened.

As I waited for the mean words to come, something else happened.
They hugged me. They let me talk and tell what was really going on in
my heart, body, and soul. Some knew exactly what I was describing,
and others sat quietly without judging.

When you are ready to share it all, there will be people ready to
listen. More importantly, God will be there waiting with open arms.

STOMP STEP

No more hide-n-seek. Face your fear and talk about your anxiety.
Remember, God is looking for you because He loves you.

PRAYER

I will not hide any longer, God. It's time
to talk to You and my parents.

JOURNAL

....

....

....

....

....

....

....

....

....

....

....

TWENTY-THREE

For God so loved the world that he gave his only Son, that whoever believes in him should not perish but have eternal life.

John 3:16, ESV

You walk into school, and a student barges in on a rampage! Desks are flipped over, papers are thrown on the floor, and every computer is broken. Destruction is happening, and the teacher is watching it all. The principal comes in and wants to know who made the horrible mess. Instead of your teacher pointing to your classmate, she says, "I will take the punishment. I love my student and even though they deserve it, the punishment will be too much for them to bear." She willingly gives up everything to show mercy.

God feels this compassionate about you only in a much bigger way. He knows every wrong you have done or will do. He knew you would not be perfect. God doesn't hold struggles against you. In fact, He knew the troubles you were going to face on this earth, including anxiety. Knowing the hard things ahead, He wanted to make sure you did not have to do life alone.

He wanted you to know, above all else, that *YOU* are loved by Him.

Our Heavenly Father did the only thing He could do to make a way for you to have a relationship and eternal life with Him. . .He gave up His one and only Son. Jesus came to die on the cross for our sins. Our Savior did this out of obedience to the Father and love for you and me.

You can continue turning the pages of each new day knowing there is nothing that can separate you from God—not even an Anxiety Elephant.

If you have never asked Jesus into your heart, today can be the day of your salvation. Confess with your mouth and believe with your heart Jesus is Lord and you shall be saved.

STOMP STEP

This will be the most important action you will ever take. If you haven't made Christ the Savior of your life, you can at this moment.

PRAYER

Dear Jesus, I believe you died on the cross for my sins. I ask You to forgive me of my sins and cleanse my heart. Come into my heart and life. I believe you are my Savior and Lord.

JOURNAL

....

....

....

....

....

....

....

....

....

TWENTY-FOUR

Can any one of you by worrying add a single hour to your life?

Matthew 6:27, NIV

Up at the plate waiting for the perfect pitch. . .but what if you miss? Strike 1, strike 2, strike 3 YOU'RE OUT.

You wait for that one list or roster to open up where you can know, without a doubt, you will make it and be the best. . .you are still waiting.

You sit and study the vocabulary over and over, worried of what might happen if you make less than an A.

You don't turn in the homework assignment pretending you don't care, but the truth is you are embarrassed because you really didn't understand what to do and you are worried about the response.

Perfection is not required to walk the journey God has for you. The worry of getting it right every single time is stealing life away from you. The good news is God knew you wouldn't get it right every time. He never put the requirement of perfection on us so you can take it off of yourself. All you need is a willingness to obey, the faith to take steps forward, baby and giant, with lots of grace.

A practical tool many counselors use is called "The Worry Box". You can create this by using a shoebox. Decorate it with anything you want from dried noodles to gobs of glitter. Cut a hole in the middle big enough for slips of paper to fit through. When worry thoughts come attacking, physically get rid of them. Write them down and throw them into The Worry Box. This visual gives you a tool to use to let go of worry so you can enjoy life the way God desires for you.

STOMP STEP

Create your own Worry Box.

PRAYER

I am giving my worries to you, Lord.

JOURNAL

....

....

....

....

....

....

....

....

....

....

....

TWENTY-FIVE

For God has not given us a spirit of fear, but of
power and of love and of a sound mind.

2 Timothy 1:7, NKJV

Fear has been one of the biggest triggers calling Anxiety Elephants to come and pick on me.

Traces of this enemy are in different moments of my life. Sleeping in the dark was a no-go for me in middle school, so I slept with a light on to stop darkness from surrounding me. Riding on roller coasters was never on my "fun list," until I met my husband. I cried on the first one we rode together—don't tell him!

Triggers signal Anxiety Elephants to show up and pick on your body, mind, and soul. Unless you are aware of what these signals are, you don't realize they have been activated until the Elephants are already beating you up.

What could trigger your anxiety? Here are some examples of common issues signaling Anxiety Elephant attacks:

- Stress level increases because of tests or peer pressure
- Lack of sleep
- Socializing or lack of socializing (isolation)
- What is going into the body and mind (food, drink, outside influences/messaging)
- A busy after-school schedule
- Social Media

Recognizing your triggers now puts the power back in your hands. By knowing ahead of time if any of these things are about to happen in your life, you can stop the sneak attack of Anxiety Elephants. Remind yourself in those moments what type of mind and spirit God has given you. Timothy makes it clear we no longer have a spirit of cowardice looming inside.

STOMP STEP

List your triggers from the list above. How can you use this information to have a sound mind?

PRAYER

Thank you, God, for reminding me I do not have a spirit of fear, and these triggers do not control me. Help me to walk in power, love, and with a sound mind.

JOURNAL

....

....

....

....

....

....

....

....

TWENTY-SIX

And we know that for those who love God all
things work together for good, for those who
are called according to his purpose.

Romans 8:28, ESV

God wastes nothing in your life. He will use it all for good, including this battle with anxiety. He takes what the enemy meant to use as negative and turns it into a positive. Through the assault of all the emotions and feelings trying to control your life, you are learning how to turn towards the Lord and seek direction from Him.

This verse reminds me of Jesus feeding the 5,000. He is surrounded by all of these people with no food. The disciples find a little boy with a small lunch containing five loaves of bread and two fish to feed the massive crowd. This young child gave all he had, and Jesus performed a miracle. Good came out of this small lunch.

As you place the anxiety which is trying to steal your life in God's hands, He will begin to do a mighty work. The tools He has placed in your hands will become natural weapons for you to use against the heavy weight of the elephant trying to do a sneak attack.

Not only has He given you power over this enemy, but He will give you an opportunity to help others. You have friends facing the same emotions, feelings, and triggers you have. They are feeling scared. God will equip you and prepare you to teach them what you learn.

STOMP STEP

Who could benefit from what you learn? Brainstorm and
pray for opportunities to share this hope with them.

PRAYER

God, Thank you for giving me tools and
guidance on how to overcome anxiety.

JOURNAL

....

....

....

....

....

....

....

....

....

....

....

TWENTY-SEVEN

Fear not, for I am with you; be not dismayed, for I
am your God; I will strengthen you, I will help you, I
will uphold you with my righteous right hand.

Isaiah 41:10, ESV

Going to bed at night made me feel jittery and uneasy. I checked under my bed for monsters and carefully examined the shadows on the wall. Finding a creative excuse to avoid sleepover parties was not easy, but I managed. Fear took fun moments out of my life.

The Anxiety Elephants never grow tired of putting scary thoughts in your brain. Fear takes what you see and manipulates it into something completely untrue.

Where have Anxiety Elephants taken your mind in fear? How do you stand your ground when fear comes?

First, begin to speak God's Word out loud and remind fear who your God is. Our scripture today is a great weapon to use. Memorize it and hide it in your heart.

Next, when fear says you can't do something, face your fear and go for it. Maybe, you are wanting to go out for an after-school team; you got this!

Finally, make friendships with other kids you can reach out to and share your fearful thoughts. You might be surprised and relieved to hear them say they are feeling the same thing.

We do not have a reason to fear since we are on the winning team. The threats of this world will never be able to destroy us or our security in Christ. Trusting in Him and trusting that He is in control and takes care of us, helps us to overcome fear.

STOMP STEP

Write today's scripture down and place it on your bathroom mirror. Pick something small you have been afraid to do and go tackle it.

PRAYER

Thank you, God, that I have nothing to fear with you on my side. Thank you for strengthening me to crush these Anxiety Elephants today. They no longer have power over me.

JOURNAL

....

....

....

....

....

....

....

....

....

....

....

TWENTY-EIGHT

"You intended to harm me, but God intended it for good to accomplish what is now being done, the saving of many lives."

Genesis 50:20, NIV

His own brothers threw him in a pit. Can you imagine? Joseph was sold as a slave by his siblings. He had no control of the events that were about to take place, but he knew he could trust in God. He ended up serving a man named Potiphar, got thrown into jail, and finally ended up in front of Pharaoh to interpret two dreams. Joseph spoke of the harvest coming and warned of the famine to follow. God used him to make sure a plan was in place to have food for everyone. He was put in charge of the whole land of Egypt as Pharaoh's second-in-command. Thirteen years later, his brothers would come to Egypt for food and Joseph was given the opportunity to serve them and reunite with his father. Our scripture today is the words Joseph spoke to his brothers when they became afraid.

What happens to you when something comes, and you can't control the outcome?

Ultimately God is in control of everything, and we can trust Him. This is good news for us. We don't have to allow worry to consume us and make us feel like we are spiraling out of control. One thing that will help when this out-of-control feeling comes is to focus on what you *can* control.

We can control our attitude, our thoughts, and the words we say. Instead of thinking of the worst-case scenario, think of a positive one. Use your words to speak about an encouraging outcome. Choose to allow your attitude to be focused on the good and not become a Negative Nelly. The rest, leave up to God.

By releasing yourself from the role of Savior-in-Chief, relief fills your heart and mind. You were never meant to control everything.

STOMP STEP

Find or create a stress ball to squeeze as
a reminder to release control.

PRAYER

Thank you, God, for being in control.

JOURNAL

....

....

....

....

....

....

....

....

....

....

....

TWENTY-NINE

Start children off on the way they should go, and
even when they are old they will not turn from it.

Proverbs 22:6, NIV

Have you ever trained for a sport? Maybe you have seen your parents work hard, preparing to run a marathon. Training is part of almost everything we do from hobbies to jobs to learning in school. Helping you build a disciplined mental muscle is a command we are given to do right now instead of waiting until you are older.

I wish I would have known I didn't have to hide at your age. What I was feeling and experiencing with anxiety was not because of anything I was doing wrong. Nothing is wrong with you.

As you turn the pages of this book, the desire behind it is to equip you now so when you are a grown-up, you will be prepared for the pressure coming your way. You can practice how to deal with things and not feel as though you need to hide them and press them down.

This is like a training manual to help you create new habits. These habits will form a new way of thinking for you so you can be prepared to knock out Anxiety Elephants when they come towards you. No longer will you be afraid of them. They will see you are no longer an easy target because you have the play-book on how to fight back in faith and in practical ways.

STOMP STEP

You are doing great as you move through every day! What have you learned to apply to your life when Anxiety Elephants come?

PRAYER

Thank you, Jesus, for helping me to learn
new skills to cope with anxiety.

JOURNAL

....

....

....

....

....

....

....

....

....

....

....

THIRTY

Do not be afraid of them; the Lord your
God himself will fight for you.

Deuteronomy 3:22, NIV

Everywhere I turned, he was there. He always made sure to find a seat close to me at church. If he saw me in the fifth-grade hallway, there was no getting away. This little boy would make fun of how I talked, how I answered questions; anything you could pick on, he did.

One day, I woke up with a painful headache. I had been experiencing headaches but nothing like this. All of a sudden, I realized my vision was blurry on the sides. Straight ahead was crystal clear, but to the right and left were little silver stars.

While at the doctor, he asked me one simple question, "Is someone bullying you at school?" I couldn't hold it in any longer. The words came out faster than I could think. My parents learned about the bullying along with the doctor. As I shared, relief came, and I could see.

I was so anxious about seeing this bully and what he would do, it caused harm to my body. Instead of telling someone, I felt pushing it down inside was easier.

This may be a hard question to answer, but is someone bullying you at school? Is it causing you to feel stomach pain, headaches, rapid heartbeat, or constant nervousness?

If you are being bullied, you have permission to tell someone. It is not wrong, and you are not being a tattletale. There are adults who want to help you.

The Lord is fighting on your behalf. With Him on your side, you can stand up to the bully. Your lips may quiver, and your words might shake, but when they see your boldness, it will make a difference.

STOMP STEP

Share with your parents or a teacher you can trust about bullying. Your children's minister will listen when you need them.

PRAYER

Dear God, give me courage to tell someone about being bullied.

JOURNAL

....

....

....

....

....

....

....

....

....

....

THIRTY-ONE

Be alert and of sober mind. Your enemy the devil prowls around like a roaring lion looking for someone to devour.

1 Peter 5:8, NIV

You and I have a real enemy.

The devil attacks because he wants you to be silent. He uses the weapon of shame. He doesn't want you to talk about the anxiety you experience and how it makes you feel. Our enemy wants you to think you are the only one, so don't bother sharing.

This tool of shame makes you feel embarrassed and small. It causes weird sensations in the pit of your stomach from mean thoughts you have about yourself. Satan runs these untrue statements through your mind to keep you hidden behind a forest of weeds so he can attack without anyone seeing.

He is a liar.

You are not the only one he uses this tactic on. What you are feeling is real. This is not made up in your head. It is a big deal, and we are not going to dismiss it and pretend to make it go away.

How can you be alert and of sober mind? Stop pressing your thoughts and emotions down. It's clogging your mind. Acknowledge what is there and what is happening inside.

Let the walls down and share your struggles with people who can help and hold you accountable. Accountability is not meant to shame you. Accountability is there to grow you and stretch you into all God has created you to be. When you are no longer isolated, your enemy will have a harder time attacking. There is power in numbers.

STOMP STEP

Write the name of one person below you
can share your struggles with.

PRAYER

Thank you, God, for the people who love me. Help me to
share my emotions and no longer push them down.

JOURNAL

....

....

....

....

....

....

....

....

....

....

....

THIRTY-TWO

For we are God's handiwork, created in Christ Jesus to do
good works, which God prepared in advance for us to do.

Ephesians 2:10, NIV

When you wake up in the morning, what are the first thoughts you say to yourself? Are you telling yourself what you are not and who you will never be? Have you forgotten how much time God spent making you and breathing life into you?

Think about this—the skillful work of our Master Craftsman created every fiber of our being. We matter so much to him, He made sure we were not a duplicate of any other person. The Lord thought about YOUR PURPOSE as He was creating you ON PURPOSE.

Your body and mind are listening. They interpret your words through actions and reactions. Negative talk breeds negative action. To see a change in your day-to-day self, change your internal dialogue. Be conscious and intentional with the words you speak to yourself.

Going from a defeatist mindset to an overcomer mindset is going to take practice. You will not get this right the first time, but repetition will be your friend. And there's no time like the present to start.

STOMP STEP

Go look in your mirror. Name characteristics you like about yourself.
It could be your hair, the way you make people laugh, anything.

PRAYER

God, I am so amazed and thankful You took your time creating me on purpose for a purpose. Help me to speak words of life over myself today and believe them.

JOURNAL

....

....

....

....

....

....

....

....

....

....

....

THIRTY-THREE

For God did not send His Son into the world to condemn
the world, but to save the world through him.

John 3:17, NIV

We all have one bully in our life who constantly puts us down. This bully speaks hateful words. It tells us all the things we should be doing because others are doing them. Bully statements like:

You should be as good a student as she is.

You should be able to do it by yourself.

You shouldn't battle anxiety.

You should be the star of the football team and not sitting on the bench.

You shouldn't fail.

Are you ready to hear who this bully is, the one attacking you?

It's **you.** We are our own worst critics. How do we stop our "should" bully?

Allow the love and forgiveness we find in Jesus to penetrate our hearts. Change any poisonous thoughts about yourself invading your mind. Combat lies with truth, and God's Word is full of the truth of who you are:

- *A friend of Jesus.* (John 15:15)

- *Accepted by Christ.* (Romans 15:7)

- *Chosen, holy, and blameless before God.* (Ephesians 1:4)

- *God's workmanship created to produce good works.* (Ephesians 2:10)

Finally, believe. Believe these things are not just true about others, but they are true for you.

It's time to silence your bully.

STOMP STEP

Every time the bully attacks, fight with TRUTH. Remind the bully exactly who you are. Don't back down. Pick one of the scriptures shared today to help you dig your heels in and fight!

PRAYER

Thank you, Jesus, for giving me TRUTH. Help me to not listen to the bully anymore.

JOURNAL

....

....

....

....

....

....

....

....

....

THIRTY-FOUR

For she said to herself, "If I only touch his garment, I will
be made well." Jesus turned, and seeing her he said,
"Take heart, daughter; your faith has made you well."

Matthew 9:21-22, ESV

Imagine you are hanging out with friends. You get hit in the face with a dodgeball, and the blood flows. Your mom runs to get a rag and tells you to hold your head back. . . for twelve years. How uncomfortable would that be? How much life would you miss out on because of this bloody situation?

The woman in our verse went through this very thing. She had a blood disease causing her to miss out on life for twelve years. No one can relate to what she is going through or understand her fear and emotions. Doctors cannot help her. Family and friends have turned their backs on her. Her culture defines her as unclean and unwanted.

Then Jesus came to her town. She heard about His miracles. She risked it all, down to her life, for a moment to reach out and touch Him. Stepping out of her mental and physical prison, she chose to believe Jesus could set her free.

Jesus was very clear when He said HER FAITH made her well. A small act of faith, even in her weakness, is what healed her. Hebrews 11:1 describes faith as having confidence in what we hope for and assurance about what we do not see. She walked towards Jesus believing He would heal her without any physical proof.

Your faith is powerful like the wind. You can't see it, but you feel it. Use faith to reach out to Jesus and believe for Him to do something amazing in your life. Faith can move mountains. Even the mountains looking like elephants.

STOMP STEP

Simply reach out in FAITH today and ask God to
heal you and help you overcome this anxiety.

PRAYER

God, I am taking a risk and asking you to do what
only You can do in my heart and mind. I am reaching
out in faith asking you to bring healing.

JOURNAL

————

THIRTY-FIVE

Trust in the Lord with all your heart, and do not lean on
your own understanding. In all your ways acknowledge
him, and he will make straight your paths.

Proverbs. 3:5-6, ESV

Confession time! I am a MAJOR control freak!

This is slightly embarrassing, but I feel like we have been through a lot over the previous pages, so why hold back now? Here goes...I will look up the ending to a movie so I can control my response! Don't worry, I don't share the ending with others and ruin it for them.

At this point you guys are either laughing at me, laughing with me, or laughing at yourself because you do the same thing!

We feel our way and understanding is right. If it doesn't go the way we think it should or if a kink is thrown into the plan, what do we do? We freak out! We panic and freely open the gate to let Anxiety Elephants come in and add fuel to the fire *WE* started.

Some of the anxiety we experience at times is because we have put ourselves in those situations.

You can take pressure off of yourself today! Not everything is supposed to be within your control. He has a better view of things for your life. You can trust in what He sees. Acknowledge Him and seek Him first. You do not have to figure it out on your own anymore.

STOMP STEP

Ask God for advice. Ask Him how He wants you to fight back when Anxiety Elephants come at you. Give Him back the controls.

PRAYER

Guide my steps, Lord. You are the Pilot of
my life. Help me to enjoy the ride.

JOURNAL

....

....

....

....

....

....

....

....

....

....

....

THIRTY-SIX

God is our refuge and strength, an ever-present help in trouble.

Psalms 46:1, NIV

The world of social media and conversations through the computer screen came to life when I was a teenager. We would all gather around our computers on Friday nights waiting to hear, *"ding!"* and three of our favorite words: You've Got Mail!

No one knew the threats sneaking through those screens. Cyber-bullying has become a real problem attacking your generation. Some of you may have experienced or are experiencing getting picked on through social media, group texts, and other platforms designed to hold the message for a few short hours and then disappear.

It may leave the app, but it doesn't leave your heart. The words are etched in your brain causing a pain difficult to explain. Online bullying affects boys and girls. Daily, mean messages go out across the world harming those your age.

God is a refuge, a safe place for you to turn to in times of trouble, like cyber-bullying. You can talk to Him about the hurtful things happening. He also wants you to talk to the adults placed in your life to help.

Maybe you are reading this, and you feel some conviction because you aren't the one being bullied but choosing to bully others. You didn't realize the harm it was causing until now. As the Holy Spirit is gently showing you the wrong actions you have taken, use this moment to do the right thing and confess.

STOMP STEP

You don't have to be silent anymore. Talk to
a trusted adult about being bullied.

PRAYER

I need help with a bully. Give me courage, Lord,
to stand strong and allow adults to help.

JOURNAL

....

....

....

....

....

....

....

....

....

....

THIRTY-SEVEN

Therefore do not worry about tomorrow, for tomorrow will worry about itself. Each day has enough trouble of its own.

Matthew 6:34, NIV

Often times, worry and anxiety come together. Worry is a symptom many experience when Anxiety Elephants attack. I wanted to see how the dictionary's definition of worry lined up with what the Bible says. Webster's dictionary says worry is mental distress resulting from concern usually anticipated; anxiety.

Through a website called BibleGateway.com, I discovered a dictionary of Bible themes and found worry. They describe worry as a sense of uneasiness and anxiety about the future. Both definitions reveal to us how our thoughts can go into worry mode when we are thinking too far in the future, trying to figure out outcomes of a scenario that probably won't happen, instead of trusting God with what each day brings.

What do you find yourself worrying about today that is in the future?

Jesus is reminding us to keep our thoughts centered on right now. What you have going on today needs your attention instead of what could be weeks or months from now.

When you find your mind going into the future, pull back by using the senses God gave you: Sight, taste, hearing, smell, and touch.

What can you see in front of you?

What can you taste?

What do you hear?

What can you smell?

What can you touch?

By doing this, it brings you back to reality.

STOMP STEP

Put your senses to work! What can you see,
hear, taste, smell, and touch right now?

PRAYER

Thank you, God, for giving me built-in
senses to bring me back to reality.

JOURNAL

....

....

....

....

....

....

....

....

....

....

THIRTY-EIGHT

But those who hope in the Lord will renew their strength.
They will soar on wings like eagles; they will run and
not grow weary, they will walk and not be faint.

Isaiah 40:31, NIV

After an anxiety attack, exhaustion sets in. You are tired and embarrassed. The hard part is no one sees everything happening inside you so they can't understand why you feel so weak.

Hope is a powerful thing in those moments. It paves the path to belief. Hope fuels an inner strength inside us we almost forgot God has placed there. This means power is there even if it's not felt instantly.

By turning to hope, we find our strength renewed to get up and go again. Just as an eagle can hold his wings out and ride on the wind with no effort, this is what hope gives us--little effort is required on our part as God carries us through.

Even if you still feel a little weary, He won't allow you to faint. When you lean on hope in the Lord, you don't need much to make it through the day. A small mustard seed will do.

STOMP STEP

Grab your parents and watch the birds in the sky. Take a
moment to see how easily they fly through the air.

PRAYER

Give me wings like eagles, Lord, in the moments I feel exhausted.

JOURNAL

....

....

....

....

....

....

....

....

....

....

....

THIRTY-NINE

Rejoice always, pray continually, give thanks in all circumstances; for this is God's will for you in Christ Jesus.

1 Thessalonians 5:16-18, NIV

I love when scripture is short, sweet, and to the point! Paul is not wasting any time in his words to the church of Thessalonica. Here, we find him giving a guide for how to live a holy life.

These three steps can make a huge difference in our day to day lives when it comes to anxiety. By focusing on rejoicing, praying, and giving thanks in all circumstances, we won't have time to think on things making us anxious.

Rejoice always, even in the not so fun situations. By looking for the good, we find it. Having a heart and mind searching for ways to enjoy life guards against the negative weighing you down.

Pray continually. Did you know you can talk to God all day? You don't have to wait to be with your parents or at church. You can be sitting at your desk at school and a thought can cause your heart to race. You can talk to God in the moment asking him to help you take deep breaths and think about something else.

Give thanks. We don't have to wait for turkey to give thanks. An attitude of gratitude is a powerful resource. When we are thinking on purpose about what we have to be thankful for, it puts a protective wall between us and Anxiety Elephants. They won't be able to break through the power of a Heavenly weapon.

Rejoicing, praying, thanksgiving. These are three simple things we can do to make a powerful change in our life.

STOMP STEP

Challenge yourself to only see the good today, even in hard things. Journal what this was like for you.

PRAYER

Dear God, help me to see the good in everything using an attitude of gratitude.

JOURNAL

....

....

....

....

....

....

....

....

....

....

FORTY

Therefore put on the full armor of God, so that when
the day of evil comes, you may be able to stand your
ground, and after you have done everything, to stand.

Ephesians 6:13, NIV

I always loved riding four wheelers with my cousin in the summer.
She was much more willing to go on adventures, allowing me to
experience fun I would have missed. One day, we decided to try and
go up a new hill. We almost made it. We got to the top, but didn't
have enough power to move forward. We flipped back to the bottom.
Luckily, we were not hurt traveling backwards down this slope.
Our helmets protected us from what could have been a dangerous
situation.

Why does a soldier wear armor? That's right, to protect themselves
in battle against attack.

God gave us this direction for armor for the same reason. One
important piece is the helmet. We wear physical helmets for lots of
things—baseball, softball, horseback riding, riding bikes, etc. If you
fall or get hit in the head, this piece of equipment protects you from
serious injury just like it did my cousin and me.

The helmet of salvation does the same for us. It protects our minds
from hurtful thoughts that could cause us serious pain. When we put
this helmet on daily, we are suiting up to protect our brains.

What is the helmet of salvation? This is our relationship with Christ.
Having salvation in Him gives us the confidence we need to stand
strong against Anxiety Elephants. Putting on this daily reminder
that we are secure in Christ means they can't take us away from our
Heavenly Father.

STOMP STEP

Grab a helmet, go for a bike ride, and remember the full armor God has given you to stand courageous!

PRAYER

Dear Jesus, thank you for the helmet of salvation.

JOURNAL

....

....

....

....

....

....

....

....

....

....

....

FORTY-ONE

Do not be conformed to this world, but be
transformed by the renewal of your mind...

Romans 12:2a, ESV

The world throws so many messages in your direction every day:

"Do this," "Hang out with these people," "Change this about yourself," "Don't mess up," "Don't tell anyone or they will laugh," "Hide," and "God doesn't care."

No wonder you feel the stomping of Anxiety Elephants all around you. Hearing so many messages can be confusing, and it is hard to distinguish between the truth and a lie.

Transforming our mind keeps us focused on truth which is from God.

When I was a kid, we watched a cartoon where old cars transformed into new, amazing machines designed to wipe out any villain coming their way. On-screen they become larger than life. The change happens in a moment, and the coolest vehicles appear with personality and swag for days. They are confident in who they are and their ability to complete the mission.

Reading God's Word can bring about this type of change. Think of it like an instruction manual. As you put each step into action, it gives you the fuel and power you need to stand against your enemy. This keeps Anxiety Elephants from coming in and twisting your thoughts. When we know the truth, the confusion the world tries to throw out doesn't get through.

STOMP STEP

Grab a Bible and discover where the book of Romans is located. Find our scripture from today and underline it. Take a look at Genesis to see how creation began. Discover the family tree of Jesus in the first few verses of Matthew. God's Word is fun to read!

PRAYER

Thank you, God, for your powerful Word.
Help me to fall in love with it.

JOURNAL

....

....

....

....

....

....

....

....

....

....

....

FORTY-TWO

Even though I walk through the darkest valley, I will fear no evil,
for you are with me; your rod and your staff, they comfort me.

Psalms 23:4, NIV

At six years old, I had surgery on my left foot. The cerebral palsy caused it to turn inward when I was born. This procedure would help turn my foot straight and change the way I was walking, but I was scared.

I forgot I wasn't supposed to eat breakfast the morning of the surgery. My bowl of cereal never tasted so good! When we arrived at the hospital, they turned us right back around and said to come the next day. . .without eating. Trying to sneak sugary goodness past your mom never works, so the next morning, we were on our way.

Rolling away from my dad on the hospital bed was hard. I screamed for him to come with me as the door shut. The nurse calmed me down and prepared a tiny kid as best as she could for the next step. When I woke up from surgery, my parents were waiting with smiles on their faces.

When shepherds are guiding their sheep on a dangerous path, they use the staff and gently put pressure on the sheep to keep it going in the right direction. This allows the sheep to sense the presence of their shepherd and know they are safe and not going alone.

God was with me during this dark time, and He is with you. His presence will bring you comfort and help you to continue forward on this journey. He tenderly moves you along much like the shepherd moves his flock.

STOMP STEP

Create a fun obstacle course for your family or friends.
Blindfold and guide them like the shepherd with his sheep.

PRAYER

Thank you, God, for guiding me on this path. Even
when it is dark, I know I can trust you.

JOURNAL

....

....

....

....

....

....

....

....

....

....

FORTY-THREE

...He said to them, "Let the little children come
to me, and do not hinder them, for the kingdom
of God belongs to such as these.

Mark 10:14, NIV

When Anxiety Elephants come, they convince you to find a place to hide. It can be easy for us to believe no one will listen because they have better things to do. The words, "Don't bother them" run through your mind a million times.

Jesus specifically says to let the little children, you guys, come to him. He says to not hinder, or stop, you. He doesn't want any person or anything, even Anxiety Elephants, to stop you from coming to him.

If Jesus was sitting face to face with you right now, what would you tell him about your anxiety?

Imagine it is you and Jesus hanging out in your room. You're eating popcorn and watching random videos. Jesus looks at you with wonder in His eyes. The crunching stops and you hit pause to start talking. Every word and thought you have held onto tightly is now pouring out.

As you talk to Jesus, He opens His arms and pulls you close. When your words are finished, it's His turn. Your Savior and Friend pours out life-giving statements where anxiety once dwelled. Grace and mercy fill your heart as He restores your soul.

STOMP STEP

Now that you have imagined hanging out with Jesus, give it a try.

PRAYER

I just want to sit and talk to you, Jesus.

JOURNAL

....

....

....

....

....

....

....

....

....

....

FORTY-FOUR

"We do not know what to do, but our eyes are on you."

2 Chronicles 20:12b, ESV

There are times you just don't know what to do when the anxiety attack comes. You try everything you have used in the past and nothing works. It feels worse. The attack is coming from all sides.

This happened to King Jehoshaphat in the Old Testament. He was getting attacked, not by one enemy, but three all at once! They had come to wage war. They were getting very close to Jerusalem and the King was stumped. He did not know what to do, where to be, or how to send out his troops. For him, his only choice was to stop and seek the Lord.

As Jehoshaphat waits, God gives His directions through a Levite man. The Lord says not to be afraid of the vast army for the battle is His (verse 15). The next day, the King sent out worshippers ahead of the army. They went praising God for His faithfulness. As they were singing, God was ambushing the enemy.

When we turn our eyes to God in anxious moments and choose to worship Him, our focus moves from what is causing us anxiety to the One who is greater than our Anxiety Elephant enemy. We can use our praise just as King Jehoshaphat did in battle.

What are some of your favorite worship songs right now? Use these anthems of praise as your battle cry against Anxiety Elephants.

STOMP STEP

Make a worship battle playlist to turn on when
the anxiety is attacking from all sides.

PRAYER

You are worthy of my praise, Lord!

JOURNAL

....

....

....

....

....

....

....

....

....

....

....

FORTY-FIVE

But he said to me, "My grace is sufficient for you,
for my power is made perfect in weakness."

2 Corinthians 12:9, ESV

I am not enough.

How could I allow myself to feel and act this way?

Why am I not trusting God?

I am a disappointment to God and to those around me.

Have you ever had ungracious thoughts about yourself? The list above includes things I told myself daily. I woke up persecuting myself and would go to bed doing the same thing. Perfection was my only option. Grace wasn't for someone like me—or so I thought.

Praise God, I was wrong.

Today's message is for all the perfectionists out there. When the goal of perfection is not reached, what happens? Who wants to give up? The enemy is good at making us feel like we will never meet the standard.

God wants you to know He has grace for you. He wants you to see yourself the way He sees you. He sees His child who desperately wants to move forward.

Instead of looking at where you are not, take a look back and see where you once were. Consider how far you've come. He will love you through this journey and get you where He wants to take you. He has not given up on you, so don't give up on yourself.

STOMP STEP

Write down some of your wins below. Take a
moment and realize you are not where you were
and celebrate the victory in where you are.

PRAYER

Thank you, God, for your amazing grace.
Help me to celebrate Our victories.

JOURNAL

....

....

....

....

....

....

....

....

....

....

....

FORTY-SIX

The Lord your God is in your midst, a mighty one who will
save; he will rejoice over you with gladness; he will quiet
you by his love; he will exult over you with loud singing.

Zephaniah 3:17, ESV

Sit and ponder today's verse with me. Go back and read it again and
put your name everywhere you see the word "you." How did the
verse become more personal and real?

"The Lord our God is in our midst." Wherever you are, He is right
there with you.

"He is Mighty, and He WILL save!" It may look like you will never get
past Anxiety Elephants and you won't ever overcome them, but those
thoughts are lies. Today's scripture shows us something different. He
is more powerful than those anxious reflections.

He is rejoicing over you with gladness! He feels great joy and delight
in you. It doesn't matter your situation or your circumstance. Your
Heavenly Father is captivated by you. He created you in His image.
Everything He created, He called good—this includes you.

He takes it one step further and exalts over us with loud singing—
not a quiet whisper. He is singing passionately and rejoicing over
each and every one of us. God's singing over you doesn't stop because
anxiety may come in.

Abba Father wants to quiet your anxiety with His love today.

STOMP STEP

Sit in God's presence. Through your prayer time,
write down what He reveals. Nothing can take away
your Father's care, not even a stinky elephant.

PRAYER

God, I humbly ask You to reveal Yourself to
me. Allow me to experience You in these quiet
moments. I am waiting to meet with You.

JOURNAL

··

··

··

··

··

··

··

··

··

··

··

FORTY-SEVEN

For he has not despised or abhorred the affliction
of the afflicted, and he has not hidden his face
from him, but has heard when he cried to him.

Psalms 22:24, ESV

In my deepest battles with anxiety, I wondered if God was there with me and if He could hear my cries. I often thought if I saw myself unworthy, He definitely saw me in the same light. I felt tired and alone. I couldn't find the strength to get up and out from under Anxiety Elephants.

Have you found yourself in this place with anxiety? Have you wondered if God hears your plea anymore? Have you thought of yourself as unworthy of help—especially His?

At this point in the journey, you may need to make a turn; an about-face from the direction you are going. Our Abba Father does not despise us or our afflictions. He isn't ignoring your appeal for help. If you are ready to make a mental shift and hear from Him, it is time to begin the cleaning-out process.

You have pressed down your troubles for far too long. By holding on to so much, there is no space available for you to hear or feel God. Maybe you didn't realize you were gripping it until now, but it's time to release it all. Once you let those painful emotions go, you will be able to hear the still small voice coming from the Lord.

STOMP STEP

Write all your troubles below. It's time to let them go.

PRAYER

Thank You, God, for allowing me to share all of my troubles.

JOURNAL

....

....

....

....

....

....

....

....

....

....

....

FORTY-EIGHT

Anxiety in a man's heart weighs him down,
but a good word makes him glad.

Proverbs 12:25, ESV

Anxiety is so overwhelming, you can't breathe. What breath you do get out is very shallow. It can be crippling. It keeps you from enjoying your life and living it to the fullest. Trying to hide the pain only gives anxiety more power.

Honestly, I thought my superpower was to keep everything bottled up and deal with it alone. My solo struggle was actually more like kryptonite.

The closer you hold anxiety to your heart, the more power you give it over you. It weakens you, crushing you little by little. Anxiety wants to isolate you because it knows if you are not around anyone else, no support or encouragement can be spoken over you.

The first step to getting out from under isolation is to verbally confess the pain you are carrying and efforts to try and fix it alone. Second, after confessing and receiving God's forgiveness, you must forgive yourself. If God can forgive you and cast the weight of guilt far, far away, you can do the same.

Third, start rebuilding your community. Maybe you have pushed friends away and closed yourself off. If so, it is time to relearn how to have friends and how to be a friend.

Prayer is the final step. You don't have to wait for someone to ask if you need prayer. You are not bothering people by requesting prayer. Family and friends love you and you matter to them. Prayer changes things, sweet friend, and it's time for things to change.

STOMP STEP

Ask someone to pray for you. I can't wait for you to feel the
freedom from allowing others to help carry your heavy weight.

PRAYER

Jesus, show me the people You have prepared
to be in my community of support.

JOURNAL

....

....

....

....

....

....

....

....

....

....

....

FORTY-NINE

When anxiety was great within me, your
consolation brought me joy.

Psalms 94:19, NIV

I decided to look up the definition of "consolation" in today's verse. Merriam-Webster's Dictionary tells us it means: the act or an instance of consoling—comfort. So, our verse is telling us when the feeling of anxiety is great, God's comfort will bring us joy.

Notice the writer of this Psalm says, "*When* anxiety was great within me." He did not say "if." He is showing us anxious thoughts will come after us. Thoughts of sorrow, pain, worry, conflict, doubt, fear.

I totally get it. I know what it is like when Anxiety Elephants appear to overpower us. I know how it feels when they paralyze you and you can literally do nothing.

BUT—I also know the other side, something I desperately want you to know, which is to feel God's comfort and His loving arms wrapped around you. His great big bear hug brings your soul such delight when you turn to His loving embrace.

At times, I resisted this solace because I didn't think I deserved it. Thankfully, God does not give us what we deserve. He gives us what He longs for us to have, and that is communion with Him. Don't resist His comfort and joy today. He loves you. The satisfaction you will find in His care will beat back any Anxiety Elephant coming after you.

STOMP STEP

Ask God to help you feel His loving arms wrapped
around you. Sit and let Him love you.

PRAYER

Dear Heavenly Daddy, I want to feel your comfort and joy when anxiety seems great. Please let me feel your loving arms around me as I sit at your feet.

JOURNAL

....

....

....

....

....

....

....

....

....

....

FIFTY

But now, this is what the Lord says…"Do not fear, for I have redeemed you; I have summoned you by name; you are mine."

Isaiah 43:1, NIV

I love the phrase *but now* in the Bible. It signals a shift is coming. Something new and different is about to happen. Change is coming in an amazing way.

For so long, Anxiety Elephants have held you down. They have bullied you, danced on you, trampled you, attacked you, and belittled you. They have stolen your joy and robbed you of living your life to the fullest. They have sucked the enthusiasm out of you. They have controlled you.

Today, it all changes.

Your *but now* moment is happening. There is a transformation taking place even as you are reading this devotional. Your spirit is rising up as you realize God is telling you exactly who you are and what to do!

Anxiety Elephants may have convinced you that you were about to burn in the flames, *but now,* God has shown you those flames cannot consume you.

Anxiety Elephants may have made you feel like you were going to drown under their pressure, *but now,* God has shown you He is carrying you through those waters and they will not overcome you.

Anxiety Elephants may have told you, you don't matter, and no one cares, *but now,* you know you are important to your Abba Father and He calls you by name.

Seize your *but now* moment today. Turn the page. Grab a hold of these truths. You are not fighting for victory, *but now,* you are fighting from victory!

STOMP STEP

Write about one thing you have changed
since beginning this devotional.

PRAYER

Praise you, Father, for my "but now"
moment. Thank you for the shift!

JOURNAL

··

··

··

··

··

··

··

··

··

··

FIFTY-ONE

Behold, I am doing a new thing; now it springs
forth, do you not perceive it? I will make a way
in the wilderness and rivers in the desert.

Isaiah 43:19, ESV

Yesterday, you had your *but now* moment. You turned the page on your old way of thinking and living. Now, it is time to walk in the new. Guess what? New is exciting but, new can be hard.

I would love to give you all warm fuzzies and make you think this is going to be a cakewalk, but I would be doing you a disservice. I am thrilled about the new happening for you, but it is going to take some work.

Continuing into the new requires doing some new things on our end. This is not a one-way street where God puts in all the effort. To walk this out, we are going to have to put work in. What does this new work look like?

If we want to experience a new and different way of living, we have to challenge ourselves in this new way of walking—stepping out in faith. It requires changing what we are doing now. Whether we want to admit it or not, our old habits have opened the door for Anxiety Elephants to come in and harass us. If we are ready to destroy them, we must take a first step of faith.

STOMP STEP

Change one thing you do in the morning to keep
walking in a new way of living. Share with a parent
or close friend to hold you accountable.

PRAYER

Lord, I know I need to make some changes and I need help.

JOURNAL

....

....

....

....

....

....

....

....

....

....

....

FIFTY-TWO

So God blessed the seventh day and made it holy, because on
it God rested from all his work that he had done in creation.

Genesis 2:3, ESV

I am so excited you have made it to this day! I am giving you permission to do something you rarely allow yourself to do. Are you ready?

Drum roll please . . .

Today, I officially give you permission to REST.

We have convinced ourselves rest is a bad thing. We have put rest and laziness in the same category. They are not the same at all. To be lazy is to avoid work or to be unwilling to work.

Resting, on the other hand, is giving yourself a moment—some time to relax and recover. Rest is needed to do the good works God created you to do. Rest allows your brain to get out of overdrive, which is where Anxiety Elephants find an open door to come in and disrupt.

Anxiety Elephants use busyness to overwhelm you and make you think you are being lazy if you aren't active with all the things, and I mean ALL the things. They have convinced us we are doing something wrong if we have any free time.

When God rested, He stopped. He was still. In stillness, He was able to look at all He had done, and He saw it was good. When we rest, we follow His example.

STOMP STEP

I have found my best rest comes when I disconnect, turning off the phone, computer, and social media. Pick one thing to disconnect from and rest today.

PRAYER

Help me to simply disconnect and rest, Lord. Thank You that rest brings restoration.

JOURNAL

....

....

....

....

....

....

....

....

....

....

FIFTY-THREE

About midnight Paul and Silas were praying and singing
hymns to God, and the prisoners were listening to them,
and suddenly there was a great earthquake, so that the
foundations of the prison were shaken. Immediately all the
doors were opened, and everyone's bonds were unfastened.

Acts 16:25-26, ESV

Anxiety Elephants (a weapon of Satan) know the power of worship.
Our adversary attacks our thoughts to strip our weapon of worship
from our hands. Satan knows praise brings breakthrough, walls fall,
victory happens, and the salvation of others can result.

Have you tried to tell Anxiety Elephants to leave you alone, only
to have the enemy attack harder? Have you ever felt like you were
thrown into a prison? Paul and Silas were tossed into a dark place,
much like the darkness we experience when anxiety casts a shadow
over our lives. The disciples could have sat in fear and let the
darkness silence them, but they chose to pray and sing to the Lord.
This knocked the walls of their cell down—and the walls of everyone
around them collapsed.

I can only speculate they were hurting and sore, but their focus was
on WHO had more power than the bars imprisoning them. If Anxiety
Elephants have beaten you up pretty good, you may feel fairly bruised
yourself. But God is more powerful than anything Anxiety Elephants
may have thrown at you. Choose to worship Him.

STOMP STEP

Choose a worship song. When you open your mouth in faith and worship the King of Kings, the earth will move. Your enemy will shake when you sing in spite of your circumstances.

PRAYER

I worship You, Almighty God. I praise You, the Creator of this Universe and thank you for your desire to have a relationship with me.

JOURNAL

....

....

....

....

....

....

....

....

....

....

....

FIFTY-FOUR

Yet it was good of you to share in my troubles.

Philippians 4:14, NIV

If you came to me with a broken arm, what would you think if I told you to cover it up with your shirt and keep playing? You would probably look at me funny; wondering why I wouldn't get you help. This is what we are doing when we hide the mental struggle of anxiety. Just like covering up a broken bone doesn't make it go away, camouflaging anxiety doesn't fix the issue.

Many people helped me through my struggle with anxiety. It was scary to tell them at first. I wasn't sure how they would respond or what actions they might take. I discovered there was no judgement as I began to open up. They reminded me often of how much they loved me and were there for me.

They all shared in my troubles in a different way. Many of my friends felt relief when I talked to them about Anxiety Elephants because they had their own. Two words brought us closer together, "Me too." We could stop pretending everything was okay around each other when it wasn't.

Professional counseling and speaking with my doctor brought me great comfort and support. They showed me how to dig up the causes of my struggle. In getting this kind of support, I was able to release the troubles I'd held in for so long. Without their help, I would have stayed stuck in the same harmful patterns. Just as seeking professional help for physical problems in our lives benefits us, doing so for our mental health is also important.

God is not upset with you for having all sorts of helpers in your life. He gifted them with the ability to serve you in this way. As our scripture reminds us, sharing the load is a good thing.

STOMP STEP

Have an open conversation about counseling with your parents. If you are interested, be honest and tell them.

PRAYER

I know longer want to hide my struggle with anxiety. God, help me to talk to those who can help.

JOURNAL

....

....

....

....

....

....

....

....

....

....

FIFTY-FIVE

Have I not commanded you? Be strong and courageous.
Do not be afraid; do not be discouraged, for the Lord
your God will be with you wherever you go.

Joshua 1:9, NIV

Joshua was a mighty warrior. He became the leader of the Israelites after Moses died. Moses is the guy God used to part the Red Sea to escape Pharaoh and his army. Can you imagine having to follow in his footsteps?

He needed some reminders from God. This was not a time to be consumed with doubt or fear. Joshua had been called to lead these people forward. It was going to take fighting some battles and facing some big enemies to get to the Promised Land.

We are only nine verses into this first chapter of Joshua. This is the third time God tells him to be strong and courageous. He wants Joshua to be this way physically but more importantly, mentally. Joshua needed to be firm in his thoughts of faith over doubt.

Anxiety Elephants will use a seed of doubt to stir a panicked moment in your heart. It grows and moves into your actions causing your legs to feel like dead weight. The rushing adrenaline needs an outlet, but you don't know how to step forward.

Joshua had to do this by keeping his thoughts grounded in faith. He refused to allow negative voices to cause confusion in his mind. He focused the adrenaline running through his veins into action by marching forward instead of being frozen in fear.

STOMP STEP

When you feel the surge coming, take action. Run
in place, do jumping jacks, or go for a walk. In those
moments, let the adrenaline burn outwardly while
your thoughts grow strong on the Lord inwardly.

PRAYER

I am choosing to keep my thoughts on you today, Lord,
to move forward and no longer be stuck in fear.

JOURNAL

....

....

....

....

....

....

....

....

....

....

....

FIFTY-SIX

In peace I will lie down and sleep, for you
alone, Lord, make me dwell in safety.

Psalms 4:8, NIV

You may be reading this devotional and the only time you experience anxiety is at bedtime. You move through your day thriving at all you do. Then, your parents tell you thirty minutes until bedtime, and panic sets in.

Being alone with your thoughts often feels like it is just you and a loud speaker in your room. These thoughts are not a whisper at night like they are in the daytime. The most random thoughts pop up. Before you know it, two hours have gone by and you are frustrated and tired. Now you are thinking, "Why can't I just turn the messages off in my brain?"

Finally, you drift off to sleep only to hear the alarm go off all too soon for a new day.

When our body and mind do not get the rest they need, it makes our brain feel more on edge. Things that normally wouldn't set you off or put you into an anxious place, are now making all the bells and whistles sound.

How can you turn the anxious thoughts off so you can turn sleep mode on?

Start your bedtime routine earlier and give your mind more time to power down. Turn the electronics off and remove them from your room so the temptation to get on your device and scroll is no longer there. Studies have shown that the blue light of your screen suppresses melatonin which helps us sleep. Blue skies by day help us be alert. Blue screens by night disrupt our sleep. By resting your eyes, you are signaling to your brain it is time to be calm and quiet.

Because we can trust that God handles our concerns, we are safe to rest. We can allow ourselves to focus on Him before we drift off to sleep so that we can remain aware of His presence with us. This paves the way to finding the rest your body is ready to receive.

STOMP STEP

My mom taught me as a child to write Bible verses on small pieces of paper and place them under my pillow. Try this powerful tool using today's scripture. By saying these words out loud, it gives your body direction on what to do.

PRAYER

Thank you, God, for caring about my sleep. I
trust you are keeping me safe tonight.

JOURNAL

....

....

....

....

....

....

....

FIFTY-SEVEN

So I commend the enjoyment of life, because there is nothing
better for a person under the sun than to eat and drink
and be glad. Then joy will accompany them in their toil all
the days of the life God has given them under the sun.

Ecclesiastes 8:15, NIV

A few miles down the road from me lives Tina the Alpaca. She enjoys big fields to run and play in with her friend, Hank the Turtle. She is either skipping around or rolling in the dirt. It's as if nothing bothers her. Well, unless you are coming towards Tina with cutting shears.

Tina enjoys life and it is evident to all the humans and animals around.

Sometimes, anxiety can cause us to want to be serious about everything. There is a pressure inside to get everything done with complete accuracy. Our schedule or to-do list is so long, there is no time for fun. If you stop for one second to laugh, you feel like you have failed because that time was wasted.

God wants you to have room for fun in your life. Yes, there is a time to work and be serious. But there is also time for joy and gladness. All of it is important and commanded by the Lord.

You are not messing up by relaxing and letting fun be added to your list. Find something you can do to bring a smile to your face. Joy helps us conquer anxiety by adding lightness to our steps. It could be as simple as taking a walk outside with your mom. You might have the best hill in the neighborhood to race down with friends. Or maybe you want to take a cue from Tina and go play in some dirt.

STOMP STEP

Go outside and play in the dirt today. Invite friends to join you!

PRAYER

Thank you, God, for showing me it is ok to enjoy
life and not be so serious all the time.

JOURNAL

....

....

....

....

....

....

....

....

....

....

....

FIFTY-EIGHT

*I sought the Lord and he answered me; he
delivered me from all my fears.*

Psalms 34:4, NIV

Summer vacation has arrived, and your family is taking a road trip. You are pumped about getting the boogie board dusted off and your toes buried in the sand. The thought of playing with your younger brother or sister has pleasantly entered your mind which never happens.

Something not so pleasant has also entered your mind—anxiety. The muscles in your legs tense up thinking about the long ride. You toss and turn, worried about the weather along the way. A racing heart is causing slight dizziness as you enter your side of the car. Snacks and activities are ready to go, but you are having second thoughts.

Have you ever felt the teasing of Anxiety Elephants while preparing for a long trip? Maybe you experience it every day getting in the car because the roads around your house can be dangerous. I remember anxious thoughts attacking me after some of my friends were in automobile accidents.

The trip will be fun once you arrive, but you need help enjoying the journey. Ask yourself why you feel a sense of nervousness when you get in the car. Wrecks can trigger these thoughts if you, or someone you care about, was involved in an accident. TV News may have recently shown a serious accident involving a teenager signaling an anxious feeling in your body.

Once you know where the Anxiety Elephants have found an open door, you can work on closing it. Be honest and talk to your parents. Ask to be included in the travel planning and look at your trip on the

GPS. Find out if there are alternate routes to use in case the interstate is at a standstill. Find some fun road trip games to play. Throw on some headphones and close your eyes for a power nap.

Before you leave, ask your family to pray for God's protection together. Confess any fears to the Lord and request freedom from this car anxiety.

STOMP STEP

Get in on the planning of your next trip. Be honest and talk to your parents about the travel part. Discuss some fun things you can do getting comfortable in the car.

PRAYER

God, help me to overcome my anxiety of traveling. Thank you for your protection.

JOURNAL

....

....

....

....

....

....

....

....

FIFTY-NINE

Though one may be overpowered, two can defend
themselves. A cord of three strands is not quickly broken.

Ecclesiastes 4:12, NIV

I was speaking in a local elementary school a couple of years ago about anxiety. After I shared my story and we practiced some coping skills together, the courage of a third grade boy still stands out. In front of the entire group, he asked: "Can you tell me how to deal with social anxiety?" I was speechless as God brought to my attention how hard it can be for you guys when it comes to social events.

It is very important to remind you at this point of our journey how helpful counseling can be if you have dealt with this issue or anything we have walked through for several months now. They can help you in a life changing way.

There are lots of opportunities coming your way to go to birthday parties, dances, sleepover parties, pool parties, concerts, and the list could go on. You want to go, but you get sweaty palms just thinking about leaving your bedroom; your safety net.

If you were honest, you are afraid to be around others outside of your normal routine. Worst case scenarios play through your mind causing you to doubt that anyone really wants you there. What if you say something silly or don't know anyone there?

Start with baby steps. Instead of saying no to everything, pick a couple of occasions to say yes. When an event comes up, talk to your friends. Find out who is going and plan to arrive together. Set a time limit so you don't feel pressured to stay the entire time. If you realize you are enjoying yourself, contact your parents ahead of time and ask to stay a little longer.

Don't allow Anxiety Elephants to keep you from fun with friends. God wants you to do life together.

STOMP STEP

What is one fun thing you can go do with friends or an activity coming up? Draw a picture of what this would look like below.

PRAYER

God, give me courage to start doing fun
things with groups of people.

JOURNAL

....

....

....

....

....

....

....

....

....

....

....

SIXTY

The name of the Lord is a fortified tower;
the righteous run to it and are safe.

Proverbs 18:10, NIV

When my parents called me by my first and middle name, I knew they meant business. When the last name came into play, trouble was coming. Do your parents ever call you by multiple names or even nicknames and you know what they mean by each?

God has different names too. Each one is a reminder of WHO He is in our life and why we can trust Him.

God is:

El Shaddai--The Lord God Almighty (Genesis 17:1)

Jehovah Shammah--The Lord is There (Ezekiel 48:35)

Jehovah Jireh--The Lord Will Provide (Genesis 22:14)

Jehovah Shalom--The Lord is Peace (Judges 6:24)

Immanuel--God with us (Matthew 1:23)

Friend--Friend of Sinners (Matthew 11:19)

Yahweh--Lord, Jehovah (Genesis 2:4)

El Roi--The God Who Sees Me (Genesis 16:13)

When you feel Anxiety Elephants coming close, call God by any of His names and He will be a strong tower. He will be a safe place to run to where you don't get trampled.

STOMP STEP

Do a quick internet search for Names of God.
Write new ones you discover below.

PRAYER

God, thank you that I can call Your name and you are listening to me.

JOURNAL

....

....

....

....

....

....

....

....

....

....

....

SIXTY-ONE

The angel of the Lord came back a second
time and touched him and said, "Get up and
eat, for the journey is too much for you."

1 Kings 19:7, NIV

Elijah straight up felt like dying. He had just made a major stand for God and saw a huge victory. Now we see him running and hiding from an evil woman named Jezebel. He told God earlier in this chapter he would rather die.

Have you ever felt like saying these words? Or have you said these words? This is a safe place to be honest. I remember telling God at one point in my life I was a burden and everyone around me would be better off if I weren't here.

Scary place to be.

God didn't allow Elijah to stay here, and he doesn't want you to stay in this place either. He encouraged Elijah to simply rest and eat. When's the last time you got a good night's sleep? Or the last time you ate a good meal with your family?

God created your body to give you cues. When we feel anxiety welling up inside, sometimes it is because our body is trying to tell us to stop and take a break or telling us it is time to eat. What is your body telling you?

STOMP STEP

Have you ever said the words Elijah spoke and felt like dying? It is time to tell your parents or an adult you feel safe talking to.

PRAYER

Help me to listen to my body cues, God. You have
me here for a reason and I want to live it out.

JOURNAL

....

....

....

....

....

....

....

....

....

....

....

SIXTY-TWO

"For I know the plans I have for you," declares
the Lord, "plans to prosper you and not to harm
you, plans to give you hope and a future."

Jeremiah 29:11, NIV

Notice this verse doesn't say, "I have a plan for you, as long as you don't struggle with anxiety."

I believed there was nothing I was going to be able to do with my life because the anxiety was so strong inside. Do you ever feel this way?

Jeremiah reminds us God has a plan for everyone. He didn't skip us or take it away because Anxiety Elephants decided to show up in our lives. His plan for you involves hope and a future. His plan also involves using this anxiety for good.

Everything in your life He will use. The anxiousness you are experiencing doesn't change what He has in store for you. The good news is we are not that powerful.

Your Heavenly Father can use the attacks you have felt to show compassion to a friend at school who is going through the same thing and feels all alone. His plan could involve you speaking out at your church about anxiety and some ways you have learned to cope.

Whatever His plan is for your life, it is good. You can trust Him with your right now and your future.

STOMP STEP

Share a dream you have for your future.

PRAYER

God, I choose to trust you with my today and tomorrow.

JOURNAL

....

....

....

....

....

....

....

....

....

....

....

SIXTY-THREE

Accept one another, then, just as Christ accepted
you, in order to bring praise to God.

Romans 15:7, NIV

I will never forget our elementary school track meet in the sixth grade. When my brother, friends, and I all discovered we got to miss the entire day of school, we all tried out! I did the high jump and 400 meter race.

Coming around the last turn, I hear a group of students chanting. To my surprise, it was my team chanting for me: "Carebear! Carebear! Carebear!" That was my nickname ...not very cool for sixth grade, but it pushed me to run harder and I ended up placing.

My friends accepted me and loved me. They knew I was different from them physically. They cheered me on even though I limped to the finish line. At that moment, I felt like everyone else. My disability did not define me.

Having friends to encourage you in hard times makes a difference.

They will be there to listen if you need to tell them about the headaches and stomachaches you feel at night because you hear your parents yelling. A friend will love on you when you feel embarrassed because you failed a test you studied really hard for. Your buddies will cheer you on when you hit the game winning shot with your heart pounding out of your chest.

Accepting one another in this loving way, brings praise to God.

STOMP STEP

How can you and your friends show kindness
towards one another today?

PRAYER

Jesus, help me to look for ways to encourage my friends.

JOURNAL

....

....

....

....

....

....

....

....

....

....

....

SIXTY-FOUR

And he said to them, "Why are you afraid, O you of
little faith?" Then he rose and rebuked the winds
and the sea and there was a great calm.

Matthew 8:26, ESV

Thunder booming.

Lightning flashing.

Rain pounding.

You peak through your fingers to see the sky light up while trying to cover your ears with the other hand. The pause lasts for thirty seconds and the storm gets closer. There is only one thing left to do:

RUN!

The pitter patter of your feet wakes your parents as they realize bad weather has caused you to feel scared. You hide under the covers until your heart goes back into your chest and your breathing slows down. The downpour is so close you can hear the power of the wind.

Thunderstorms feel creepy, don't they? You are not alone in coping with Anxiety Elephants coming out to play during dangerous weather. It is common for people of all ages to feel anxious when they see a threatening forecast. In your area, you may have hurricanes, blizzards, or tornadoes.

What can we do when storms pop up? How can we not allow the anxious thoughts to take over?

Have a plan. Know where you will go if the weather does get dangerous. Keep a flashlight by your bed and a favorite cuddle close. Remind yourself your parents will do everything they can to keep you safe. When you hear the loud noises and the hard rain, remember you can call out to Jesus. Ask Him to give you peace and calm in the storm.

If you need to have a sleeping bag ready, just in case to go to your parents room, that's ok too.

STOMP STEP

Create a Stormy Weather Plan with your parents.

PRAYER

Thank you for your protection during stormy weather, Lord.

JOURNAL

....

....

....

....

....

....

....

....

....

SIXTY-FIVE

For the word of God is alive and active. Sharper
than any double-edged sword, it penetrates even
to dividing soul and spirit, joints and marrow; it
judges the thoughts and attitudes of the heart.

Hebrews 4:12, NIV

I have never seen a sword with a double edge, but I can only imagine how cool it would be! A double-edged sword could cut through anything around it trying to attack.

The Bible is a powerful resource in the process of overcoming Anxiety Elephants.

When the enemy comes charging towards you, fight back with God's Word because it is truth. Truth is greater than any deceiving word, including the lies Anxiety Elephants use to hold you back.

God gave us His Word as a weapon to help us push back against the negative words attacking our minds. When we focus on His message, it allows us to remember the facts.

How can you use God's Word as a sword to strike down Anxiety Elephants when they attack in your mind?

Change the words you are hearing by the words you see. Videos you watch, books you read, and songs you listen to can lift up or tear down. Adding worship music, switching to age-appropriate media, and reading devotions like this one will help aid in this shift you are making.

The hurtful echoes between your ears will be silenced with life-giving encouragement you view in the handbook God gave us thousands of years ago we call the Bible. His thoughts have never changed about you nor has His Word. Keep your eyes on His message that has stood the test of time. This is one sharp object you will always be allowed to touch.

STOMP STEP

Grab colorful paper or notebook paper. Write down some of your favorite scriptures and tape them all over your walls.

PRAYER

Dear God, Help me remember how powerful the Bible is for my life. Thank you for giving me this sword.

JOURNAL

....

....

....

....

....

....

....

....

....

SIXTY-SIX

Above all else, guard your heart, for
everything you do flows from it.

Proverbs 4:23, NIV

We are friends right? We have gone through a lot together. I have shared parts of my story, and I hope you have found courage to talk about some things you have experienced. We have looked at God's Word, laughed and maybe even cried. Now comes the time where I may share something you won't like. I am going here because, as your friend, I want you to know the truth.

Here we go...social media is not the best place to get direction for life. I will not tell you to get off of it completely if you are there, BUT, I will ask you to consider pulling back for a moment.

So many confusing messages happening through video, chat, and memes. How do you know which one to listen to? They change constantly every day and with all the filters you have no idea who anyone is. These platforms are pumping messages into your heart and mind telling you what to do to make yourself better and accepted.

Some of you may even be experiencing the hurtful side of social media because you are being bullied through the DM's. You are sent painful videos constantly and cannot get away.

Taking a break from these platforms will remove the pressure of this world which is causing your breath to weaken and your heart to feel crushed.

If social media has attacked your heart and mind, walking away from it for a season is not a defeat. It is a victory in God's eyes worth celebrating.

STOMP STEP

One day. Take one day off of social media and journal how it went.

PRAYER

I am surrendering my social media to you, God.

JOURNAL

....

....

....

....

....

....

....

....

....

....

....

SIXTY-SEVEN

Moses said to the Lord, "Pardon your servant, Lord. I have
never been eloquent, neither in the past nor since you have
spoken to your servant. I am slow of speech and tongue."

Exodus 4:10, NIV

Fun fact for you guys. Public speaking is the number one fear of
adults. I thought it might be spiders, snakes, or heights. Standing
in front of people staring at you, in a quiet room, being judged or
graded on what you say is actually scarier for most people.

How do you feel about standing up to speak in front of your
classroom? Do you feel your palms sweating onto your paper? Do
your thoughts leave your head before you even get out of your desk?
Do you try to force the words, but a stutter comes out instead?

Moses was nervous about speaking in front of people too. He had
trouble getting the words out and it took him longer to say things.
God knew this about Moses, but He still commanded him to go to
Pharaoh and demand he let the Israelites go.

God reminded Moses He was the One who created our mouths, and
He could help him say exactly what needed to be said. The Lord
sends Moses a helper, his brother Aaron, but God also taught Moses
how to speak and trust He would do the work. Moses only needed to
be obedient.

When you get ready to speak in front of people, know you are not
the only one who feels a little anxious. Moses has been in your shoes.

Take a good deep breath before you talk. Find a spot on the back wall
right above a friendly face. Let the words flow naturally instead of
at a racing pace. Practice with family or in a mirror. Ask God to help

you speak through the nerves. The more you do it, the more your confidence will increase and your new courage will help you get past the fright.

STOMP STEP

Practice giving a sixty second speech in front of your mirror.

PRAYER

God, just as you helped Moses, give me the
words to speak in front of others.

JOURNAL

....

....

....

....

....

....

....

....

....

....

SIXTY-EIGHT

"I have told you these things, so that in me you may
have peace. In this world you will have trouble.
But take heart! I have overcome the world."

John 16:33, NIV

If only I could tell you your life is going to be rainbows and unicorns. No struggle, no pain, no bullies, no rejection, no hard things, no more Anxiety Elephants. We will experience life like this one day in heaven, but here on earth, Jesus is reminding us we will have trouble.

Trouble looks different for everyone, but for some trouble comes in the form of anxiety. It can block your thoughts, making it difficult to focus on school work, causing nervousness to the point you are afraid to be around others, and make your body feel weird things inside.

Jesus is with us in our troubles. We can have hope knowing He has overcome the world! This means He has already won.

How do you take heart when you feel anxiety coming? You can pray and talk to the Lord in that moment. Use this scripture to remind yourself you are not messing up because trouble has come. Remember, you are on the winning team! You are playing kickball against Anxiety Elephants and the undefeated Team Captain is up to the plate. They do not win, so you can breathe a sigh of relief.

When you experience trouble, don't forget, Jesus told us we would. Stand up tall with your shoulders back and your head up. He chose to fight for you, and we know He never loses.

STOMP STEP

Jesus can help us defeat trouble by giving peace, giving courage, and even giving creative ideas! List below ways He has helped you defeat the trouble anxiety has caused you.

PRAYER

Thank you for fighting for me, Jesus!

JOURNAL

....

....

....

....

....

....

....

....

....

....

....

SIXTY-NINE

If you faint in the day of adversity, your strength is small.

Proverbs 24:10, ESV

For the first time in her life, my daughter was trying out for a team. The night before the roster posted, something was bothering her. She stood in the doorway silent. I told her over and over, "There is no pressure. There is no pressure from your Dad or me or your friends." I could barely get the last word out when she looked down.

It felt like God stopped me in my tracks to ask if *she* felt pressure. She began to tell me the pressure she felt inside thinking about not being good enough. Her thoughts went to what if her friends made it and she didn't. The stress of having to try out for something was getting to her. As I listened to her words, I had to apologize for dismissing what she felt.

How can you stand strong through the adversity you face? What can you do if you are trying out for a team, taking an important test, or moving to a new city and the pressure is getting to you?

Acknowledging there will be difficulty in life helps keep Anxiety Elephants from causing you to faint. Have a plan to be prepared for the days of adversity. Include in this guide names of people you can reach out to. Write down a Bible verse that helps you to not give up. List practical steps you have learned, like deep-breathing, to put into action.

Stand strong by remembering all you can do is your best and trust in the Lord with the rest. He will not allow you to go through any difficulty alone.

STOMP STEP

Write your plan of action for adversity.

PRAYER

Heavenly Father, when adversity comes, help
me to breathe and stand strong.

JOURNAL

....

....

....

....

....

....

....

....

....

....

....

SEVENTY

I lift my eyes up to the mountains--where does
my help come from? My help comes from the
Lord, the Maker of heaven and earth.

Psalms 121:1-2, NIV

In football, the quarterback can't hike, throw, catch, and block, all at the same time. Each player has a role. The team works together and helps one another get to victory.

HELP is not a four letter word...yes I know it has four letters, but what I am trying to say is it is not a bad word. For some reason, it gets treated this way. Our culture has applauded doing everything by yourself and not "needing" others to pitch in. It has pushed this message despite the pressure and sense of failure we feel when some of us realize we can't do it all on our own.

Our verse shows us we don't have to do things all by ourselves.

Asking for HELP is one of the best things you can do to stomp out anxiety. Letting friends and trusted adults in removes the heavy load you are carrying. For example, if you were moving boxes full of shoes and clothing from your room up to the attic, how much faster would you finish and get outside to play if you asked for help?

The Maker of heaven and earth is ready to help. God's hands were meant to carry the biggest boxes you have been trying to drag across the floor. Your hands were created to let them go.

STOMP STEP

You are not weak or doing anything wrong by using these four powerful letters. I'm challenging you to put this word in action today. Know when you allow yourself to say it, HELP is on the way.

PRAYER

God, I am asking for HELP.

JOURNAL

....

....

....

....

....

....

....

....

....

....

....

SEVENTY-ONE

May the God of hope fill you with all joy and peace
as you trust in him, so that you may overflow
with hope by the power of the Holy Spirit.

Romans 15:13, NIV

In a strange way, I felt comfortable in anxiety, doubt, and fear. Even though the attacks were painful, after all Anxiety Elephants were stomping all over my chest, it was scary to choose hope. It felt safer in the pit of darkness versus reaching out for something I didn't think I deserved. Avoiding the journey leading to hope let me pretend as though everything was fine. Or at least, normal.

God is putting a stop sign in the middle of your avoidance journey today. He wants to not just give you enough hope, but give you an overflow. The only thing to avoid now is actual avoidance.

There may be several things causing anxiety inside you. Avoiding all the issues does not make them go away. It does open the door for them to grow bigger and move into other areas of your life.

Avoiding avoidance can be done by being honest about where you are at the moment. Do the Anxiety Elephants make you feel scared? Are you angry or frustrated? Does the urge to run away pass through your thoughts?

It is okay to say any of these things out loud. By having this starting point, you know how to move forward.

God is not avoiding you. As you go through this trial, have courage to follow His lead. By facing it head on, you are looking the Anxiety Elephants in the eye and showing them you will no longer back down.

STOMP STEP

Face it. Say out loud what you have been avoiding for a long time.

PRAYER

No more avoiding Lord. I'm ready to tell you everything.

JOURNAL

....

....

....

....

....

....

....

....

....

....

....

....

SEVENTY-TWO

As for me, I call to God, and the Lord saves me. Evening, morning, and noon I cry out in distress and he hears my voice.

Psalms 55:16-17, NIV

David is the writer of this Psalm. As he begins, his words are different from what we read in our verses above. David shares how his thoughts are troubling him and how anxious he feels as he finds himself surrounded by enemies. He was all alone and only God was with him.

How do you feel when you are alone? When you have to leave your parents and walk into school or church by yourself, do you feel anxious being away from them? Do your thoughts go to a troubling place like David when you are separated for any amount of time?

What can you do in those moments of separation?

Talk to your parents about the fear or sadness you feel when it is time to get dropped off for school. Be honest about the thoughts you have in your head. These thoughts may feel scary, like being worried they will get in a wreck and not pick you up. It could be you are concerned you might be forgotten and have no way of getting home. Being specific will help them understand your pause before getting out of the car.

Have a plan of what to do if your ride is running late. Memorize a cell phone number you can contact. Tell a teacher and they will help. Take a good deep breath focusing on what you want to share about your day when your ride shows up.

Cry out to the Lord as our verse directs any time of the day when those anxious thoughts over being away from family creep in.

STOMP STEP

Talk to your parents about how you feel when you are not with them. Decide together things you can do to stay away from anxious thoughts while you are separated.

PRAYER

God, thank you for reminding me I am never alone.

JOURNAL

....

....

....

....

....

....

....

....

....

....

....

SEVENTY-THREE

Therefore go and make disciples of all nations, baptizing them in the name of the Father and of the Son and of the Holy Spirit.

Matthew 28:19, NIV

It was the first time I had ever heard the waves and stood in the big, blue water. My best friend had invited me to go on her family vacation to the beach. I couldn't believe my mom was totally fine with me leaving for a week, but I didn't wait for her to change her mind! We had the best time eating junk food and staying up way past our bedtime.

At church, we had been talking about witnessing to our friends about Jesus before this trip. They handed out these square pieces of paper called tracts, and encouraged us to share the Good News of the Gospel. My friend was not in church anywhere, so I wasn't sure if she was a Christian. I tucked this card away in my suitcase just in case.

One night, my heart started beating like a drum. I knew God wanted me to talk to my friend about Jesus and ask if she was saved. The Anxiety Elephants felt so loud in my ears. I didn't know what her answer would be or what would happen after I shared. Through the fear and anxiousness, the Holy Spirit helped me. My legs were shaking by the time I was done. She didn't get mad or make me catch a bus home. A few years later, she did ask Jesus into her heart, and she lives every day to bring glory to Him.

It is normal to feel anxious about sharing your faith with your friends. Not knowing what will happen can be scary. God simply asks you to go. He will take care of their response. By pushing through the rumblings, you are showing Anxiety Elephants you care more about your friend's salvation than anything they can throw at you.

STOMP STEP

Write down the name of a friend needing to hear the Gospel. Ask God to give you courage to witness to them.

PRAYER

God, help me to share your salvation message. Please bring my friends into a relationship with You.

JOURNAL

....

....

....

....

....

....

....

....

....

....

SEVENTY-FOUR

If we are thrown into the blazing furnace, the
God we serve is able to deliver us from it, and
he will deliver us from Your Majesty's hand.

Daniel 3:17, NIV

Shadrach, Meshach, and Abednego were best buds and they loved God with all their hearts. Being asked to bow down and worship fake gods was not happening with them, even if it meant being killed in a fiery furnace. They trusted God. It helped them knowing they had each other to go through this scary time.

Can you imagine being thrown into a real fire? These three young men did get tossed into the blazing inferno. It was so hot, it killed the soldiers launching them in! A miracle happened to our young friends. Not one hair was scorched. Their clothes had no burn marks. There was no campfire smell following them around. When we roast marshmallows we smell like smoke for days and yet not one hint of fire remained on them. Not only did this happen, but Jesus came and stood in the fire with them! The king could not believe there were now four men walking in the fire.

Who are two friends you have that will share the fire you are going through with Anxiety Elephants? By doing life together, you can get through the hard things knowing God is with you and will help see you through every step. It helped Shadrach, Meshach, and Abednego to ▮▮▮▮▮▮▮▮▮▮▮ scary situation.

▮▮▮▮▮TEP

▮▮▮ around a fire or an oven
▮▮▮ of God's faithfulness
▮▮▮ fire with you.

PRAYER

Thank you, Jesus, for standing in the fire with me.

JOURNAL

....

....

....

....

....

....

....

....

....

....

SEVENTY-FIVE

You, dear children, are from God and have
overcome them, because the one who is in you
is greater than the one who is in the world.

1 John 4:4, NIV

You have permission to stomp on Anxiety Elephants like bubble wrap!

Have you ever done this? The noise is satisfying and the feeling of tiny bubbles disappearing beneath your feet makes your entire body giggle! My tweens love when we have packages delivered so they can get all the bubble wrap out and go crazy with making it pop. The dog is not as big a fan, but they could spend all day making this commotion.

God gives you the power to fight back. Our scripture tells us since the Holy Spirit is inside of us, we are able to stand firm against our opponent. You can be strong in your words and say, "NO, not today Satan!"

The enemy uses something to distract everyone. Since Jesus is greater, that makes you greater and stronger than the devil. He is under your feet. Go ahead and crush him like bubble wrap!

STOMP STEP

Two words: Bubble Wrap! Pop it with your hands or
under your feet to calm the anxiousness inside.

PRAYER

Dear God, help me remember I am an overcomer!

JOURNAL

....

....

....

....

....

....

....

....

....

....

....

SEVENTY-SEVEN

Don't let anyone look down on you because you
are young, but set an example for the believers in
speech, in conduct, in love, in faith and in purity.

1 Timothy 4:12, NIV

You have so much to offer this world right now. Being a world changer is not reserved for adults only. In fact, I believe you guys can bring about a much greater change than we! Your ability to impact your community and those around you is not restricted by anxiety you bravely face. Yes, you read the word brave because it is a brave task you take on to get up over and over and try again.

The cool thing is Jesus sees you as you will be, not where you are right now. Struggles don't define you which means anxiety doesn't get to say who you are or what your life will look like. Jesus already did that.

You can make a difference in others' lives. There are kids your age dealing with what you are dealing with and you may be the only one who can understand. God has given you hope to spread.

Maybe you feel Him gently nudging you to share your testimony at your school's Bible club or church. By standing up and sharing what is helping you with overcoming anxiety, you will give them courage to do the same.

You are prepared to set a powerful example. God will give you everything you need at just the right time. Go in faith, courage, and love. You have got this, and God's got you.

STOMP STEP

You can do this. Talk to a ministry leader
about sharing your testimony.

PRAYER

Heavenly Father, help me to share the testimony you have given me.

JOURNAL

....

....

....

....

....

....

....

....

....

....

....

SEVENTY-EIGHT

And all are justified freely by his grace through
the redemption that came by Christ Jesus.

Romans 3:24, NIV

Has anxiety told you that you don't deserve to come out of the yucky place where you are? Thankfully, God does not give us what we deserve but what He wants us to have.

He wants you to have love, joy, peace, and His grace.

Grace is a gift He gave not because we deserve it or because we earned it. God gave it freely through Jesus on the cross. Long before you and I entered this world, He knew we were going to need lots of help and forgiveness. Our Heavenly Father also wanted to give us sweet reminders of the unconditional love He has for us.

Look around you outside. How different are the trees, birds, bugs, and butterflies?

God put this beauty everywhere not because He owes it to us to see it every day, but because He wanted us to have something showing His amazing love in a different way every day. This gift of creation was given to you and me revealing how precious we are to Him.

Looking upon His handiwork outside gives you a chance to breathe in fresh air and clear your mind to get out of the weeds where Anxiety Elephants want to keep you. As you stare at the clouds, think on this gift of grace. It will never be taken away from you.

STOMP STEP

What do you see in the clouds? Take some time to look up
and find creative shapes in the pretty, white fluff above.

PRAYER

I am grateful for all the beauty you gave me to see, Lord.

JOURNAL

....

....

....

....

....

....

....

....

....

....

....

SEVENTY-NINE

For we know that our old self was crucified with him
so that the body ruled by sin might be done away
with, that we should no longer be slaves to sin.

Romans 6:6, NIV

Is anxiety a sin?

Well, not the anxiety, but the way we deal with it can be. There is a
camp for kids called CentriKid, and they give a great explanation of
what sin is: "Simply put, sin is the bad stuff we do that makes God sad
and separates us from Him." This could be something like stealing a
book from your classroom, yelling at your brother or sister, lying to
a teacher, or disobeying your parents.

When Anxiety Elephants attack, we can choose to respond in a way
that doesn't cause us to sin. Instead of hiding it, we can tell someone.
Choosing to pray in place of worrying about future events stomps
out anxious thoughts. Creating new habits, versus returning to the
old ones causing us harm, will set us free from sinful behaviors.

God is not mad at you because Anxiety Elephants are picking on you.
We can see from our verse we no longer are bound to their tricky
plans to keep us down. You are not a slave to what you have always
done when the panic enters your heart and mind.

Change is hard, but it will help you to live in a free way. Some experts
say it takes twenty-one days to create new habits. This is only the
beginning. It took lots of days to get into the habits you have right
now, so don't give up on the process if it takes you a while to create
new ways of thinking and living.

STOMP STEP

What is one thing you want to start doing when panic tries to enter your mind? Write it down to commit to this new habit.

PRAYER

Please help me work on this new habit to bring change in my life.

JOURNAL

....

....

....

....

....

....

....

....

....

....

....

EIGHTY

"See, I have chosen Bezalel son of Uri, the son of
Hur, of the tribe of Judah, and I have filled him with
the Spirit of God, with wisdom, with understanding,
with knowledge and with all kinds of skills."

Exodus 31:2-3, NIV

Bezalel had a pretty important job: building the Ark of the Covenant.

The Ark of the Covenant held the stone tablets with the Ten Commandments written on them by God, and the Mercy Seat was crafted to sit on top. Once a year, the high priest would enter the inner part of the tabernacle to sacrifice an animal as a payment for the sins committed by the people. When Jesus came, He became the ultimate one and done sacrifice for the forgiveness of our sins.

Bezalel was filled with all kinds of skills. His skills were not like others around him. Without these abilities, he would not have been part of this project. How horrible would it have been if Bezalel had neglected his skills because he was comparing himself to others?

There are times Anxiety Elephants can cause us to compare ourselves to others and feel "less than." Playing this comparison game will steal your joy. This is one competition you can quit and walk away from today.

Think about it like this—if puzzles only had outside pieces, we would never know what the entire picture looked like. Every piece is needed. If one is missing, it doesn't work.

If your unique gifting was not walking this earth right now, there would be an empty space.

STOMP STEP

Write about one thing you can do really well.

PRAYER

Thank you, God, for making me in a unique way.

JOURNAL

....

....

....

....

....

....

....

....

....

....

....

EIGHTY-ONE

Peace I leave with you; my peace I give to you...Let not
your hearts be troubled, neither let them be afraid.

John 14:27, ESV

The world feels scary sometimes. If your parents watch the news,
you may hear what is happening while you are eating your pop tart
before school in the morning. You get to school or practice, and your
friends are talking about the bad things happening in their life. The
anxiety you woke up with is clogging your mind and the last thing
you feel is peace.

In fact, anxiety has robbed you of peace. This precious thing was
stolen, and you want it back. You don't want to walk around nervous
and on edge, afraid you might explode at any moment.

Jesus said he left peace with us so how can we walk in it?

Ask your parents to turn the news off while you are getting ready for
school and tell them the reason behind your request. Do you need
to change where you hang out on social media? If you find yourself
feeling frustrated, down in the dumps, or angry when you finish
scrolling, this is not a place providing you calm and safety.

The most important thing you can learn is to talk to Jesus. Tell him
the troubles in your heart and ask him to fill those places with peace
which leads to trust amid crazy circumstances. He is ready to hear
from you any time of the day. It can be at night when sleep doesn't
come or at school in the bathroom stall. No matter the time or place,
Jesus is ready to meet you with peace.

STOMP STEP

Talk to your parents about the news you are hearing.
Ask them questions and share what troubles you.

PRAYER

Thank you, Jesus, for peace in troubling times.

JOURNAL

....

....

....

....

....

....

....

....

....

....

....

EIGHTY-TWO

Children are a heritage from the Lord,
offspring a reward from him.

Psalms 127:3 NIV

The day has finally come where you can officially tell your parents you really are a reward because God says you are! What would be your idea of a great reward? Mine would be a trip to a theme park with cool rides, no lines, and all the pizza and ice cream I want!

God wants you to see yourself the way He sees you. Your Heavenly Father does not identify you by your struggle with anxiety. We know by our verse He thinks you are pretty valuable.

All throughout scripture, the Lord reminds us we are chosen, sons and daughters, heirs, and this list could go on and on. He gave these descriptions long before we were created. These words were penned knowing the struggles we would have and the mistakes we would make. And yet, He calls YOU a reward.

Anxiety Elephants don't take away who you are. You are precious in the sight of God. They might try to convince you only others are rewards, but now you know the truth. God packaged you in a unique way with incredible gifts and talents waiting to burst out of you.

Anxiety doesn't get to take that away from you.

STOMP STEP

Write or draw below your ideal reward.

PRAYER

You see me as a gift. Help me to do the same, Lord.

JOURNAL

....

....

....

....

....

....

....

....

....

....

....

EIGHTY-THREE

I no longer call you servants, because a servant does not know his master's business. Instead, I have called you friends...

John 15:15a, NIV

Did you know God considers YOU a friend? How cool is that?! To know the God of this Universe wants to be friends with you is kind of a big deal. You are pretty special to Him.

He wants to spend time with you and build a friendship. It's not all about rules and guidelines, but getting to know Him and sharing all of you without holding back. God likes for us to bring the good, the bad, and the ugly to Him. We can come to Him as we are, in the same way we would when hanging out with friends, talking and laughing all night long. Nothing is off limits. It is the same with the Lord. He has so much to share with you. And he wants you, as his friend, to have the freedom to share everything with Him.

Have Anxiety Elephants caused you to feel like you have to hide because there is no way God would want to be friends with someone like you having a hard time with something like them?

God doesn't see these things in you; He sees YOU.

He loves YOU.

He believes in YOU.

He is not mad at YOU.

He called you friend, and this will never change. Allow Him to be the friend you have always wanted.

STOMP STEP

Invite a friend to church then head out for some ice cream afterwards. As you hear God's Word together, think on how He calls you both a friend.

PRAYER

Thank you, God, for being my friend.

JOURNAL

....

....

....

....

....

....

....

....

....

....

....

EIGHTY-FOUR

When I said, "My foot is slipping," your
unfailing love, Lord, supported me.

Psalms 94:18, NIV

Falling down is embarrassing, but falling down in front of people is the worst! I was walking through a store with a friend, and they had just mopped the floors. Thankfully, I was behind her. We were on a mission, so this was not a slow stroll. Suddenly, I took a big step and my foot slipped. Somehow, I did not fall, but I could feel the cringy look on my face as my arms flailed in the sky. She turned around, just as I caught myself, not knowing what happened. Unfortunately, the people behind me got to see it all go down.

Anxiety does this to us. We can be walking along, enjoying life and, all of a sudden, it pulls our feet out from under us. We slip, wondering if anyone sees what is happening. The label of being a failure consumes our thoughts.

Falling down or making a mistake does not make you a failure; it makes you human. Jesus knew we were going to have slips and falls so He came to give support. This scripture reminds us even in these slippery moments, the Lord is backing us.

Once you get the hang of your footing, you will recognize the slippery spots much earlier. And if you should slip, get back up, dust yourself off, and keep walking towards your destination. A slip may slow you down, but it won't take you out.

STOMP STEP

Ask your parents to share about a time they fell in public.

PRAYER

You are the greatest supporter that I have,
Jesus. Thank you for loving me.

JOURNAL

···

···

···

···

···

···

···

···

···

···

EIGHTY-FIVE

And let us consider how we may spur one
another on towards love and good deeds.

Hebrews 10:24, NIV

Growing up, there was a place called the Mission of Hope my friends and I loved to serve. At Christmas time, families in need would come and we would get to walk the children around to pick out a new coat, shoes, and toys. Watching their faces light up helped us put things going on in our lives in a new light.

Helping others, when you are struggling, is a powerful thing. It takes the focus off whatever is hard you are experiencing and opens the door to love and good deeds possible in your part of the world. Inviting others to join you in doing these good deeds makes it more fulfilling.

I know things may be difficult for you right now. Life is throwing you curveballs right and left. Anxiety can take over and cause you to laser-focus on what you are facing and see nothing else.

But how can you challenge yourself to help someone who is going through something hard themselves and needing help?

By searching for a way to do good deeds, it takes your flashlight off your struggle and puts a spotlight on helping others. This will fill your soul with joy and gladness and bring a smile to God's face as you obey His Word.

STOMP STEP

Is there a family in need around you? Is there a student who could really use some friends in their life? What is an action you and your friends could take together to serve your community?

PRAYER

Open my eyes to see the needs of others. I want to serve You by serving them.

JOURNAL

....

....

....

....

....

....

....

....

....

....

....

EIGHTY-SIX

Submit yourselves, then, to God. Resist the
devil, and he will flee from you.

James 4:7, NIV

For years, my daughters begged for a dog. We gave them the same reasons you've heard to not get a pet:

- Too much responsibility
- No one home to take care of it
- No one will play with it

Sound familiar?

Their persistent asking finally worked. We brought home a mini golden-doodle named Cooper Hashbrown. This twenty-five pound ball of fur thinks he is the most ferocious animal on the face of the planet. He will bark his head off, warning of danger, if you get close to him. His form of attack is to lick you to death.

His bark is worse than his bite.

This reminds me of our enemy, the devil. He comes at us loud, trying to intimidate us with the thud of Anxiety Elephants pushing further and further into our space. Satan wants us to think we are no match for them.

When we submit ourselves to the Lord, it helps us to take action and resist the attack of the enemy. Resisting turns us in the opposite direction of where the devil wants you to go.

Because we have God on our side, we are more powerful than the devil! His bark will never make it past God's bite.

STOMP STEP

When the devil tries to tell you to worry, doubt, or be fearful—
RESIST—trust God, go in faith, and don't be afraid.

PRAYER

Thank you, God, for showing me I am more
powerful than the enemy through you!

JOURNAL

....

....

....

....

....

....

....

....

....

....

EIGHTY-SEVEN

You were bought at a price. Therefore
honor God with your bodies.

1 Corinthians 6:20, NIV

Did you know tens of thousands of thoughts enter your mind every day? These thoughts come so fast we don't realize they are there. Thoughts fill our brain from TV, social media, friends, teachers, parents, church, music, and yourself.

We often talk about how to honor God through our body. How we treat our bodies with the things we eat and activities we pursue is important. But it hit me; we need to acknowledge the mental part of glorifying God, not merely the physical.

I have a question: does a thought lead to an action or an action lead to a thought? The way I look at it is a thought is like a seed. You water it the more you think on it and it will eventually sprout into an action.

What do you want to think on? What does God want you to think about?

Just as we don't eat junk all day because it would give us a stomach ache, if we let all the bad thoughts in, this can cause pain through anxiety attacking us. When an anxious thought tries to enter your mind, stop and ask yourself, "Is this going to honor God if I let it stay?" If the answer is no, change the words seeking entry into something bringing glory to God.

STOMP STEP

Let's practice. Today, instead of thinking, "What if I fail this test?", shift to, "I am prepared and ready to go." The beauty of practice is it doesn't make you perfect—it makes you better.

PRAYER

I want my thoughts to make you happy, Lord. Help me to pay attention to what I let in today.

JOURNAL

....

....

....

....

....

....

....

....

....

....

....

EIGHTY-EIGHT

Each of you should use whatever gift you have
received to serve others, as faithful stewards
of God's grace in its various forms.

1 Peter 4:10, NIV

We each have received a gift. Those gifts will shine brightest through the broken places of our lives. Where God heals us, we experience His love, grace, mercy, and forgiveness. We can serve others best through understanding where brokenness can take a person, and in turn, how God can take the person through it.

Because of the broken areas anxiety brought about in my life, I experienced healing I didn't realize I needed. I began to feel compassion the way Jesus had compassion. He gave me a gift of hope and restoration. I wanted those who battle Anxiety Elephants to know the gifts available to them. I had to share what I'd learned.

Open your gift. God has given you a story. He didn't give this for you to keep to yourself. He gave it to you because there is someone out there who needs to hear from you. They too, may think they are the only ones who get trampled on by Anxiety Elephants. They may believe this is the way life is meant to be. There are people waiting for you to share your gift with them.

STOMP STEP

Share your gift—story. Write it here first to help you.

PRAYER

Give me courage to share my story, Lord. Thank You for giving me hope. Help me to share with others who are searching.

JOURNAL

....

....

....

....

....

....

....

....

....

....

EIGHTY-NINE

They triumphed over him by the blood of the
Lamb and by the word of their testimony...

Revelation 12:11a, NIV

Will you ever completely overcome your Anxiety Elephants? The answer is: YES, you will. . . it just takes time. God's healing needs to infiltrate the places Anxiety Elephants have made their camp in for so long.

Today's scripture tells us how to overcome: by the blood of the Lamb and the word of our testimony.

Jesus did His part. He shed every drop of His blood on the cross for you and me. Now, it's your turn. There is someone out there who needs to hear about your struggle with anxiety. They need to hear how you are overcoming and how you are conquering anxiety. They need hope.

What I am challenging you to do is help someone else. Share your testimony. Your story offers healing. If you see a friend struggling, let them know you understand and care. If you see someone post on social media, send a message of encouragement.

Think about it like this—where would you be if no one was willing to help and share with you? You can do this. God will help you. Now is your time to overcome.

STOMP STEP

Look for one person you can share how God has brought you
healing. Ask God to give you the words others need to hear.

PRAYER

Thank you, Jesus, for doing your part willingly for me. Help me do my part and share the testimony you have given me.

JOURNAL

....

....

....

....

....

....

....

....

....

....

....

NINETY

Therefore, there is now no condemnation
for those who are in Christ Jesus.

Romans 8:1, NIV

The message has been somewhat similar over these ninety days of insights into God's power and love. As each page was turned, you encountered particular themes at least once—you are not alone. God hears you, there is hope, and Anxiety Elephants can be defeated. You read multiple times about the importance of seeking help, journaling, accountability, faith, prayer and worship.

Why would I include similar messages over and over?

Because reminders are needed! Anxiety Elephants have pushed their agenda into your mind and soul longer than you may want to admit. If they keep reciting the same message of fear, shame, and judgment, we are going to need to listen to the echoes of hope on a regular basis. Why do we think we only need to hear once there is no condemnation in Christ Jesus? Even the shampoo bottle instructs us to "lather, rinse, and REPEAT".

Zig Ziglar said it best, "People often say motivation doesn't last. Well, neither does bathing, that's why we recommend it daily."

I love this statement! We take baths daily to stay clean. We brush our teeth every day to keep our teeth strong and prevent stinky breath. If we do these tasks daily to help our body, shouldn't we also have daily habits cleansing our minds and souls?

You are now equipped with scripture, tools, and weapons to daily silence the ridicule and disapproval from the Anxiety Elephants voices. You won't always go through a battle, but you always need to be prepared. That's how Anxiety Elephants got in to begin with—they caught us off guard.

You are ready. Keep stomping out Anxiety Elephants. They are no match for God's children.

STOMP STEP

As you close this devotional, Write out how you want to continue to grow in your relationship with God. Sign it, date it, and surrender your commitment to the Lord.

PRAYER

Thank you, Father, for all the things I have learned and the weapons you have given me to stomp out Anxiety Elephants every day.

JOURNAL

....

....

....

....

....

....

....

....

CONCLUSION

Well, you made it!

You are now able to identify your triggers and know what to do when, and if, Anxiety Elephants attack. You discovered scriptures speaking directly to your heart and helped you recall God's truth, so you are ready when Anxiety Elephants try to knock you down. You held on to stomp steps you can apply to your life to deal with a sneak attack. You journaled and wrote down feelings you have locked inside.

Freedom. You found freedom.

God has equipped you with everything you need for battle. Stand strong and remember you are not fighting alone. We are waging war next to each other, for each other, and with each other. You've got this. Keep stomping my friend!

ABOUT THE AUTHOR

Caris Snider is a Christian Communicator who shares the hope of God through speaking, writing, coaching, and leading worship. She is the author of *Anxiety Elephants 31 Day Devotional.* Her passion comes forth as she shares from her experiences of overcoming depression, anxiety, fear, and shame. Caris desires to help people of all generations see their value and worth through the eyes of the Lord. It is important to her to encourage everyone to grow in their faith and mental health. Caris offers inspiration to those who feel purposeless to discover their God-given calling no one else can accomplish. For more information about Caris, her ministry, books, or speaking, go to: carissnider.com.